The Gest of Robyn Hode

The Gest of Robyn Hode

edited by Robert B. Waltz

Waltz, Robert B. *The Gest of Robyn Hode*.
Windsor, NJ: CAMSCO Music, 2012. Print.

© 2012 by Robert B. Waltz

CAMSCO Music
145 Hickory Corner Rd., E. Windsor, NJ 08520
www.camscomusic.com

Loomis House Press
www.loomishousepress.com

ISBN 978-1-935243-94-6

Book design by Robert B. Waltz
Cover design by Mark F. Heiman; Woodcut from an early printing of the Gest.

To Martha Galep
without whom this probably
would not have been finished

ἀγαθοὶ οἱ δύο ὑπὲρ τὸν ἕνα,
οἷς ἔστιν αὐτοῖς μισθὸς ἀγαθὸς
ἐν μόχθῳ αὐτῶν·
ὅτι ἐὰν πέσωσιν, ὁ εἷς ἐγερεῖ
τὸν μέτοχον αὐτοῦ.
— *Ecclesiastes 4:9-10 LXX*

Table of Contents

Preface 1
Introduction 2
   The Sources and Audience of the Poem 2
   The Setting of the "Gest" 4
   The Date of the Poem 5
   Reconstructing the Text 7
   Chronology 11
Summary: The Plot of the Gest of Robyn Hode 13
A Critical Text of the Gest of Robyn Hode 16
   The Text of the Gest 107
   The Early Copies 108
   The History of the Prints and Their Relationships 110
   Comparing the Texts: Printers, Dates, and Ancestry 121
   The Stemma, or Family Tree, of the Prints 126
   Notes on the Text of the "Gest" 128
   Divergences from Child's text of the "Gest" 139
Bibliography 141
Endnotes 144

Illustrations

   The Textura 95 Types of Richard Pynson and Wynken de Worde 119
   The Stemma of the Prints of the "Gest" 127
   The Extent of the Prints of the "Gest" 128

Preface

Francis James Child's *The English and Scottish Popular Ballads* contains about forty ballads or ballad-like pieces about Robin Hood. "The Gest of Robyn Hode" is not only the longest and most important of these, it is the longest ballad by far in Child's collection — so long, indeed, that it should properly be called a romance, not a ballad. It is also the single most important source for the legend of Robin Hood, particularly as the legend existed in the fifteenth century.

To this date, there has never been a comprehensive linguistic, textual, and historical study of the "Gest." This would probably require seven parts: an introduction to the Robin Hood legend, a discussion of the historical problems of the "Gest," a detailed commentary on the "Gest," a full critical edition of the Middle English text, a modernized version, textual notes, and a vocabulary study. This edition tries to set the groundwork by establishing a new text based on a stemmatic method — the first such text ever published. In addition to the Middle English text, it offers a modernized parallel, a limited textual discussion for the specialists, and an introduction hinting at some of the materials which might be in the larger edition..

I have had many discussions with textual critics over the years, of whom Michael W. Holmes and Stephen C. Carlson are the most important. I also owe thanks to the members of the Ballad-L mailing list. Dr. David Engle made suggestions about the presentation. Martha Galep supplied personal support and information about horses. Ed Cray and Dick Greenhaus encouraged publication of the book; Ed also offered suggestions as to the content. My parents, Dorothy and Fred Waltz, supplied financial help. Thanks also to Catie Jo Pidel and Ken Bloch.

Introduction

It is a rare man who can make a name for himself that lasts across the years. It is still rarer for a name to make a man. Yet that is what happened with Robin Hood.

It appears that by 1250 at the latest, the name "Robin Hood," or some close variant ("Robehod," "Rabunhod") was commonly used as a name for un-apprehended criminals. But none of these early mentions is substantial. Our earliest significant records of the great outlaw are the songs and poems, of which the "Gest of Robyn Hode" (#117 in F. J. Child's ballad collection)[1] is the longest and most complete.

The Sources and Audience of the Poem

There is little question that the "Gest" is a combination of older elements. The parallels to the romances of Fulk FitzWarren, Eustace the Monk, Hereward the Wake, and Gamelyn are covered in most discussions of the "Gest."[2] Less attention is paid to a series of parallels to the tale of King David of Israel as told in the Biblical books of 1-2 Samuel. Like Robin, David was regarded as a mannered outlaw — according to the Bible, David never raided Israel, but only Geshurites and Girzites and Amalekites and other non-Hebrews.[3] He remained loyal to his king, having refrained from killing Saul when he had the chance.[4] Like Robin, David was famous for piety. Given the frequent references to the Virgin Mary in the "Gest," and the "miracle of the Virgin" that is a key motif of the first half,[5] we should probably pay close attention to these parallels to the Bible and religious legends.

The fact that the "Gest" draws on so many sources hints that it is something new. This something new has caused scholarly uncertainty. The audience of the earl Robin Hood tales has been much debated. The first line of the "Gest" calls on "gentilmen" to listen to it,[6] yet follows that up by speaking of those of freeborn blood — more likely to be a reference of yeomen and guildsmen than the aristocracy or gentry.

Dobson/Taylor declare that "'yeoman minstrelsy' remains the most appropriate description for the Gest" as well as the two other earliest Robin Hood poems[7] — but they hardly explain the term. Similarly, "the Robin Hood ballads may represent the assertion of a yeoman ethic,"[8] but we don't know what this ethic is except a push for greater rights.

Dobson/Taylor conclude that "in the last resort it is the differences between Robin Hood and his counterparts rather than their similarities which deserve most attention."[9] Robin, they point out, shows no desire to take a high place in the social hierarchy. He is proud to be a yeoman. It is likely that the hearers of the "Gest" were also proud to be yeomen.

Holt believes the legend as a whole was addressed to the various clerks and other officials of feudal households, many of whom would have borne the title "yeoman."[10] Yet he also notes that Robin Hood plays were at least known to, and very likely performed before, the Pastons,[11] who were of the gentry. He also has a throwaway comment that the tales were targeted to "young men without responsibility" (this on the basis of the lack of women in the early stories).[12]

Ohlgren suggests that the audience of the "Gest" was the rising class of merchants and guildsmen:[13] "another ideological subtext promotes the interests of the London guilds by portraying Robin as a cloth merchant. The poem, I believe, was originally commissioned in the mid-to-late fifteenth century… [for use] at the election dinner of one of London's major cloth guilds."[14]

The one thing all these editors seem to agree on is that the Robin Hood legend, despite its early date and wide expression, is not an aristocratic legend. The French-speaking nobility of England perhaps had their own epic in the tales of King Arthur. And one aspect of the Arthur legend, the (oh-so-English) tales of Sir Gawain, does seem to have influenced the Robin Hood legend — or, rather, they may well have sprung from a common source. Robin's refusal to eat dinner before something interesting happens (stanzas 6-7 of the "Gest") is also found in *Sir Gawain and the Green Knight* as well as the fragmentary romance of *The Turk and Gawain*. Gawain, like Robin, has a strong reliance on the Virgin Mary.[15] *The Turk and Gawain* hints at a hitting game such as the "pluck-buffet" of Stanza 424 of the "Gest."[16] More than half the tales of Gawain "begin with a forest episode."[17] Hahn suggests that these were interludes to let the audience settle into their seats — but it would be no great stretch to create a romance which never left the greenwood. Such a romance requires a new sort of hero — and a new set of themes. The courtly love, magic, monster-fighting, and elaborate politics of the aristocratic romances are missing. Instead, we have the themes of archery competition, good fellowship, conflict with the clergy, and outlawry. If the result is less than perfect poetry, it is at least very distinctive.

The Setting of the "Gest"

In the "Gest," Robin meets the King — and that king is named "Edward." Although many have argued for other kings, the King Edward of the "Gest" gives every evidence of being King Edward II. We can sum up this evidence under very many particulars:

1. A king during a crusading period (stanzas 56-57)
2. A king who used distraint of knighthood (stanza 45, which refers to making knights by force)
3. A king during whose reign high clerical officials were known to have been robbed by outlaws
4. A king during whose reign longbows were a common weapon

5. A king during whose reign longbows were used but not widely encouraged
6. A king during whose reign social unrest would encourage outlawry
7. A king named Edward (stanza 353)
8. A king went to the north of England and was concerned with deer herds (stanzas 357-358; as was shown by Hunter long ago, only Edward II fits this description)
9. A king who lived during the period of problems with livery (stanza 107)
10. A king who would be relatively likely to personally deal with ordinary outlaws (stanzas 408, 424, etc.). Edward II liked ordinary occupations such as wall-building and hedging and ditching,[18] and hung around with common people — a very rare trait among kings of this period.
11. A king in whose reign a sheriff would be powerful but not a noble
12. A king who spoke English as well as, or instead of, French

The Date of the Poem

Since the "Gest" seems to refer to the reign of Edward II (1307-1327), we must assume it was written later. But how much later? If the "Gest" is not contemporary with the events in it, when was it written?

The dating of the poem remains a matter of controversy. Gutch claimed a date from the time of Chaucer, or the reign of Richard II (1377–1399) or Henry IV (1399–1413), which is not quite the same thing, but close.[19] Chambers thinks he can detect signs of fourteenth century language in the "Gest."[20] Child rejected this but left room for a date *c.* 1400. Knight/Ohlgren reject even this[21] — but their argument that the poem cannot have had a long life in manuscript is not compelling.

Even if we allow for the possibility of rewrites to modernize the language, the "Gest" is unlikely to be earlier than the fourteenth century, simply because the saga of Robin Hood seems to be known exclusively to the English and English-speaking Scots.[22] Given that the poem is clearly the work of a professional composer, this requires a date after English was reasserting itself as a language of the middle and upper classes, which can hardly be before 1300.

Vocabulary isn't much help. Clawson tried to use inflexional endings as a dating hint,[23] but his data would allow almost any period prior to about 1450. There are a few strange words in the "Gest," but they are no hint to date because we don't know their meaning! Nor are there many words which changed their usage between the fourteenth and fifteenth centuries. We do note that there is no mention of the office of ranger, an office probably instituted in the early fourteenth century and known to have been in existence in 1341[24] — but there is little mention of the older office of forester, either, so that's no help.

Ohlgren at one time argued that the original was made in the reign of Henry V (1413–1422) or the first reign of Henry VI (1422–1461).[25] In his later writings, Ohlgren seems to have reconsidered this dating. He strongly urges a date toward the end of the Yorkist period, choosing 1483 as a somewhat arbitrary approximation.[26] This is extremely late, given that Ohlgren is arguing that Pynson's first printing was from around 1495. Although the primary texts of the "Gest," by de Worde and Pynson, are similar enough to have a recent common ancestor, they are also defective enough that it is hard to believe the original could be only twelve years old at the time Pynson printed it!

I think we are forced to admit that we don't know the date of the final editing of the "Gest," but it is probably fifteenth century, although very likely with older components. If it were much older than the second quarter of the fifteenth century, given the northern base of the legends, it would probably be much harder to understand.

The "Gest" is almost certainly not the earliest surviving Robin Hood poem. "Robin Hood and the Monk" [Child 119] and "Robin Hood and the Potter" [Child 121] both appear to have been copied in the fifteenth century. Some of the other chronicle references appear to refer to lost ballads. But the "Gest" appears to be the first real attempt at a Robin Hood collection. And it was a major inspiration for later works — not just "popular" works but other ballads. "Robin Hood's Death" [Child 120], one of the best of the ballads, is a fuller version of the events at the end of the "Gest." "Robin Hood and the Golden Arrow" [Child 152] builds on an incident in the "Gest." This list could easily be multiplied. Authors from the fifteenth century to the twentieth have mined the "Gest" for their plots. Knowing it is essential to understanding the history of the Robin Hood legend.

Reconstructing the Text

Although usually classified as a ballad, the "Gest" is properly a romance, and clearly was compiled by one individual, almost certainly in the fifteenth century. That means that there was certainly an original version, now lost, which scholars must reconstruct. This is my attempt at a reconstruction.

Detailed notes on the reconstruction follow the text. Textual wonks are referred to this section. But the basic principle is this: Beginning with Child, editors have started with a "copy text" — that is, an edition of the "Gest" that they follow unless they have some strong reason to do otherwise. Child and his followers generally chose to use the so-called "Lettersnijder edition," which Child referred to by the symbol **a**. And yet, Lettersnijder is an abominably poor piece of printing, scarred with many errors. It is certainly not fit to be a copy text.

The alternative is to use an "eclectic" method — to take the two major editions (Lettersnijder and de Worde) and compare them, and choose whichever reading is superior. And, since both have many defects and Lettersnijder is incomplete, we must occasionally be content to emend the text.

A pair of examples may show how the difference between "copy text" and "eclectic" methods affects the "Gest." The first involves one of Robin's most important followers. In the de Worde edition of the "Gest," and its followers, he is called something like (William) Scathelock. In the Lettersnijder edition, he is (William) Scarlok.

In the copy text method, one uses the best available text unless there is strong reason to abandon it. Child used Lettersnijder as a copy text where it is extant, de Worde as a copy text where Lettersnijder fails. As a result, he uses the name "Scarlok" in stanzas 4, 17, 61, 68, 74, 77, 83, 208, but "Scathelock" in 293, 402, 435.

We do not know the original reading, but surely it was *the same* in all instances! So we must decide between "Scarlok" and "Scathelock" and adopt it in all instances. I chose "Scathelock" because it is supported by one of the fragments (**d**) as well as by de Worde. I am by no means confident of this — but I *am* confident that his name did not change simply because some pages were lost from a printed copy of the poem!

The second instance is in stanza 53, where the son of Sir Richard is reported to have slain a knight from Lanc.... Was it a knight of Lancaster? Or of Lancashire? Lettersnijder reads "Lancaster," and Child follows it. But de Worde has "Lancastshyre." The **c** fragment reads "Lancasesshyre." Surely a printer, confronted with the reading "Lancastshyre," would be tempted to correct it either to "Lancaster" or "Lancashire." No printer whose text read "Lancaster" would change it to "Lancastshyre." What's more, the **c** reading seems to presuppose "Lancastshyre." So the de Worde reading is much more likely to be original. This is the principle used throughout: the best way to edit a text is to examine and weigh all the sources, with the best reading chosen on a case-by-case basis.

The pages below show both my reconstructed Middle English text and a semi-modernized version, intended to serve in the place of a gloss. The Middle English text is in roman type; the modernized text in *italics*.

The stanza numbers on the left of each page correspond to those in Child's edition. In the several cases where I have found it necessary to break one stanza into two, the added stanza will be marked "A," e.g. 135A, 268A.

The Middle English text on the left-hand side of the page is critically reconstructed — that is, it is based on comparing the various prints and trying to determine what is the original. Most of the time, we are pretty sure of the text — when the prints agree and the reading the offer makes sense, there isn't much reason to question it. But sometimes the prints disagree, or their consensus reading is improbable. These readings are marked in **bold type**. Most of the textual data needed for these determinations can be found in Child; I hope someday to elaborate this in a full critical edition and apparatus. Some of the most important variants in the text are discussed below; these variants are marked *.

Parallel to this is a modernization of the "Gest." This is not really in modern English; it is a rather weak Middle/Modern English hybrid. But it should get the meaning of the text across, and it's easier than glossing. I have put a few readings in [brackets] where they represent radical emendations.

Most of the prints of the "Gest" do not distinguish i/j and u/v; the use of these letters has been conformed to modern orthography and such changes are not noted. Spacing between words also seems arbitrary at times and has occasionally been modified. Punctuation is editorial (although to some extent derived from Child).

Chronology

The chronology below shows historical events, events relevant to the history of Robin Hood literature, and the events in my reconstruction of the "Gest's" history of Robin Hood. The latter are shown in **BOLD**. Understand that these are not actual historical events, just the date pegs possibly used in the "Gest."

1189. Richard I King of England

c. 1193. Date John Major claimed Robin Hood was active.

1199. John King of England.

1216. Henry III King of England.

1266. Date Walter Bower claimed Robin Hood was active.

1272. Edward I King of England.

c. 1285. Date Andrew Wyntoun claimed Robin Hood was active.

c. 1293. **Birth of Robin Hood, in Lancashire or Yorkshire.**

May 22, 1306. Edward II and others **(Sir Richard?)** made knight

1307. Edward II King of England.

1314. Battle of Bannockburn.

1315. The Great Famine. **Robin in Barnsdale by this time.**

c. 1316. **Robin Hood ransoms Sir Richard at the Lee. The payment of the loan may just possibly have happened on April 3.**

1322. Battle of Boroughbridge. **Edward II in north of England.**

1323. **Robin Hood joins Edward II's court.**

1324. **Robin Hood leaves Edward's court to return to Barnsdale.**

1326. Overthrow of Edward II.

1327. Edward II deposed and killed. Edward III King of England.

1345. **Death of Robin Hood at Kirklees.**

1346. **Battle of Crécy. Men of Robin's former band likely took part.**

1377. Richard II King of England. Approximate date of the "B" version of *Piers Plowman,* the first literary mention of Robin Hood.

1399. Richard II deposed. Henry IV King of England

1413. Henry V King of England.

c. 1420: Andrew Wyntoun refers to Robin in Inglewood and Barnsdale.

1422. Henry VI King of England

1439. Piers Venables compared to Robin in a petition to parliament.

c. 1445: Walter Bower refers to Robin as a "famous murderer."

1460. Battle of Wakefield.

1461. Battles of Ferrybridge. Battle of Towton. Henry VI deposed. Edward IV King of England.

c. 1468. Sundry hints of Robin Hood tales in the Paston Letters.

1469. Robin of Redesdale's rebellion, possibly inspired by Robin Hood stories

1470. Edward IV deposed; Henry VI restored.

1471. Henry VI re-deposed and killed. Edward IV restored.

1483. Death of Edward IV. Edward V succeeds but is never crowned. Richard III King of England.

1485. Battle of Bosworth. Henry VII King of England.

1501. Gavin Douglas mentions Robin and Gilbert of the White Hand.

1509. Henry VIII King of England

1515. Henry VIII sees a Robin Hood performance

1521. John Major dates Robin Hood to the reign of Richard I.

1534. Death of Wynkyn de Worde gives absolute last possible date for the first printing of the "Gest."

1598. Anthony Munday is paid £5 for a Robin Hood play.

1663. First of the Robin Hood garlands.

Summary: The Plot of the Gest of Robyn Hode

[The First Fit.] When we begin, Robin is with Little John, Much the Miller's Son, and Will Scathelock, sending them out to seek a "guest." They are to use no force, but bring him back to dinner.

The three outlaws spy a downtrodden knight along the road. They bring him back to Robin, who serves him a fine meal — but then demands that the knight pay. The knight admits that he has only a few shillings. Robin orders John to search his baggage. John determines that it is true. Asked how he came to be so poor, the knight reveals that he has mortgaged all his lands to the Abbot of St. Mary's in order to go bail for his son. The reckoning is due, and he cannot repay, and if the Abbot will not extend the loan, all the knight's lands will be lost.

Robin and his band are moved with pity. Robin offers to pay the debt, if the knight will give surety. The knight can give none except the Virgin Mary. Robin, out of love for the Virgin, at once accepts. He gives the knight four hundred pounds, and offers Little John as a servant.

[The Second Fit.] The abbot of St. Mary's is at dinner, happily contemplating the thought that he will soon have the knight's land. The knight shows up in poor clothing and begs the abbot for more time. The abbot refuses. The knight pulls out the four hundred pounds and stalks out, ruining the abbot's day.

[The Third Fit.] Little John takes part in an archery contest, and wins easily. The Sheriff of Nottingham takes him on as a servant. A year later, when the sheriff is out hunting, John fails to get his dinner — and attacks the butler. He then fights the cook. The fight is a draw, and John invites the cook to join Robin's band. The cook agrees, and they head off to the greenwood after robbing the sheriff's home. The sheriff himself is

tricked into Robin's lair by John, where he is made to spend a night in the cold, eat from his own stolen plate, and promise to be Robin's friend.

[The Fourth Fit.] It is time for the knight to repay his debt to Robin. He starts on his way to Barnsdale — but he is delayed on his way by a wrestling. While this is going on, Robin sends out his men to find another "guest." This time, they catch a monk and his company heading for London to complain about the knight. Most of the company flees, but John and the others bring the monk, and his baggage, back to Robin. The monk claims to have relatively little money, but John searches the bags and finds that he has eight hundred pounds. Whereas the knight had been honored because he told the truth, the monk is punished because he lied. Robin confiscates the eight hundred pounds. When the knight arrives to pay back the four hundred pounds, Robin declares that the Virgin Mary has already repaid the loan, and gives the knight the four hundred pound excess.

[The Fifth Fit.] There is another archery contest in Nottingham, and this time Robin competes and wins the prize. But he and his men are recognized and forced to flee. Little John is injured in the fight. The band is forced to take refuge at the castle of the knight, now revealed to be Sir Richard at the Lee.

[The Sixth Fit.] Sir Richard is still under siege, but calls on the sheriff to consult the king. The siege is lifted, and Robin returns to the greenwood — but the sheriff then traps Sir Richard and prepares to take him away. The knight's wife appeals to Robin, who rescues Sir Richard and kills the sheriff, calling him a betrayer of the oath he earlier took. The knight, however, cannot return to his castle; he joins Robin in the forest.

[The Seventh Fit.] King Edward decides to take matters into his own hands and deal with Robin Hood himself. He comes north, but cannot find Robin. At last it is suggested that he enter the forest in disguise. The king agrees, and his party puts on the clothing of monks. Robin and his band waylay them — but eventually recognize the king and beg pardon. The king grants it.

[The Eighth Fit.] The king sets out for Nottingham, bringing Robin and his band with him. There is panic in the town, but the King agrees to take Robin into his service. Robin tries to cut a great figure at court, but after a year, his money is gone and most of his men have deserted him. He asks the king's leave to visit a chapel he had built in Barnsdale. The king grudgingly gives him leave to depart for a few days. Robin returns home and takes up his life in the greenwood. After twenty-two years, he feels old and ill, and goes to Kirklees to be bled. Instead of being cured, he is bled to death by the prioress and her lover Sir Roger of Doncaster. The poem concludes with a pious wish for the soul of Robin, who "dyde pore men moch god" ["did poor men much good"].

A Critical Text of the Gest of Robyn Hode

[The First Fytte]   **The First Fit**

1. Lythe and listin, gentilmen,   *Stop and listen, gentlemen,*
   That be of frebore blode;   *Who are of freeborn blood;*
   I shall you tel of a gode yeman,   *I'll tell you of a good yeoman,*
   His name was Robyn Hode.   *His name was Robin Hood.*

2. Robyn was a prude outlaw,   *Robin was a proud outlaw,*
   Whyles he walked on grounde   *While he walked on ground;*
   So curteyse an outlawe as he was one   *So courteous an outlaw as he was*
   Was never non founde.   *Was never yet one found.*

3. Robyn stode in Bernesdale,   *Robin stood in Barnsdale,*
   And lenyd hym to a tre;   *And leanéd on a tree;*
   And bi hym stode Litell Johnn,   *And by him there stood Little John,*
   A gode yeman was he.   *A good yeoman was he.*

4. And alsoo dyd gode **Scathelock**,*   *And also did good Scathelock,*
   And Much, the **miller's** son;   *And Much, the miller's son;*
   There was non ynch of his bodi   *There was no inch of his body*
   But it was worth a grome.   *But it was worth a pound.*

5. Than bespake Lytell Johnn   *At that time spoke up Little John*
   All untoo Robyn Hode: *All unto Robin Hood:*
   Maister, **an ye** wolde dyne betyme   *Master, if you would dine on time,*
   It wolde doo you moche gode.   *It would do you much good.*

6   Than bespake hym gode Robyn;
     'To dyne have I noo lust,
     Till that I have some bolde baron,
     Or som unkouth gest.

7   [....]*
     That may pay for the best,
     Or som knyght or **some** squyer
     That dwelleth here bi west.'

8   A gode maner than had Robyn;
     In londe where that he were,
     Every day or he wold dyne
     Thre messis wolde he here.

9   The one in the worship of the Fader,
     And another of the Holy Gost,
     The thirde **was** of our dere Lady,
     That he loved allther moste.

10 Robyn loved our dere Lady;
     For dout of dydly synne,
     Wolde he never do compani harme
     That any woman was in.

11 'Maistar,' than sayde Lytil Johnn
     And we our borde shal sprede,
     Tell us wheder that **we** shal go
     And what life we shall lede.

Then up spoke good Robin;
    "To dine have I no lust,
    Till that I have some bold baron,
    Or some unknown guest.

['We shall await some bold abbot]
    That may pay for the best,
    Or some knight or some squire
    That dwells here in the west.'

A faithful style had Robin then;
    In the land where that he were,
    Every day ere he would dine
    Three masses would he hear.

The one in worship of the Father,
    Another of the Holy Ghost,
    The third was of our dear Lady,
    That he loved yet the most.

Robin loved our dear Lady;
    For fear of deadly sin,
    Would he never harm a company
    That any woman was in.

'Master,' then said Little John
    Before we our board shall spread,
    Tell us where that we shall go
    And what life we shall lead.

The Gest of Robyn Hode

12 'Where we shall take, where we shall leve,   'Where we shall take,
    where we shall leave,
Where we shall abide behynde;   Where we shall abide behind;
Where we shall robbe, where we shal reve,   Where we shall rob,
    where we shall reave,
Where we shal bete and bynde?'   Where we shall beat and bind?'

13 'Thereof no force,' than sayde Robyn;   'Never use force,' then said Robin;
'We shall do well inowe;   'We shall do well enough;
But loke ye do no husbonde harme,   But look you do no farmer harm,
That tylleth with his ploughe.   That tilleth with his plow.

14 'No more ye shall no gode yeman   'No more shall ye [rob] a good yeoman
That walketh by grene-wode shawe;   Who walks by the greenwood shaw;
Ne no knyght ne no squyer   Neither a knight nor a squire
That **wolde** be a gode felawe.   Who would be a good fellow.

15 'These bisshoppes and these archebishoppes,   'These bishops
    and these archbishops,
Ye shall them bete and bynde;   Ye shall them beat and bind;
The hye sherif of Notyngham,   The high sheriff of Nottingham,
Hym holde ye in your mynde.'   Let him not slip your mind.'

16 'This worde shal be holde,' sayde Lytell Johnn   'This word shall be kept,'
    said Little John
'And this lesson we shall lere;   'And this lesson we shall fear;
It is fer dayes; God sende us a gest,   It's late in the day;
    God send us a guest,
That we were at oure dynere!'   That we may be at our dinner!'

17 'Take thy gode bowe in thy honde,' sayde Robyn;   'Take your good bow
                                                                                                               in your hand,' said Robin;
   'Late Much wende with the;   'Let Much go with thee;
   And so shal Willyam **Scathelocke**   And so shall William Scathelock
   And no man abyde with me.   And no man abide with me.

18 And walke up to the Saylis,   And walk up to the Saylis,
   And so to Watlinge Strete   And so to Watling Street
   And wayte after some **unketh** gest,   And wait after some unknown guest,
   Up chaunce ye may them mete.   By chance you may them meet.

19 'Be he erle, or ani baron,   'Be he earl, or any baron,
   Abbot, or ani knyght,   Abbot, or any knight,
   Bringhe hym to lodge to me;   Bring him to lodge to me;
   His dyner shall be dight.'   His dinner shall be right.'

20 They wente up to the Saylis,   They went up to the Saylis,
   These yeman all thre;   These yeoman all three;
   They loked est, they loked weest;   They looked east, they looked west;
   They myght no man see.   They might no man there see.

21 But as they loked **in** Bernysdale,   But as they looked in Barnsdale,
   Bi a derne strete,   Down a hidden street,
   Than came a knyght ridinghe;   Then came a knight riding;
   Full sone they gan hym mete.   Full soon they did him meet.

22 All dreri was his semblaunce,   All dreary was his semblance,
   And lytell was his pryde;   And little was his pride;
   His one fote in the styrop stode,   His one foot in the stirrup stood,
   That othere wavyd beside.   The other waved beside.

The Gest of Robyn Hode

23 His hode hanged in his iyn two;   *His hood hung in his two eyes;*
   He rode in symple aray;   *His clothes were a poor array;*
   A soriar man than he was one   *A sorrier man than he was one*
   Rode never in somer day.   *Rode never in summer day.*

24 Litell Johnn was full curteyes,   *Little John was full courteous,*
   And sette hym on his kne: *And set him on his knee:*
   'Welcom be ye, gentyll knyght,   *'Welcome be ye, gentle knight,*
   Welcom ar ye to me.   *Welcome are ye to me.*

25 'Welcom be thou to grene wode,   *'Welcome be thou to greenwood,*
   Hende knyght and fre;   *Gracious knight and free;*
   My maister hath abiden you fastinge,   *My master has waited fasting for you,*
   Syr, al these oures thre.'   *Sir, all these hours three.'*

26 'Who is thy maister?' sayde the knyght;   *'Who is thy master?' said the knight;*
   Johnn sayde, 'Robyn Hode.'   *John said, 'Robin Hood.'*
   'He is a gode yeman,' sayde the knyght,   *'He is a good yeoman,' said the knight,*
   'Of hym I have herde moche gode.'   *'Of him I have heard much good.'*

27 'I graunte,' he sayde, 'with you to wende,   *'I agree,' he said, with you to go,*
   My bretherne, **all** in fere;   *My brothers, together here;*
   My purpos was to have dyned to day   *My purpose was to have dined today*
   At Blith or Dancastere.'   *At Blythe or Doncaster.'*

28 Furth than went this gentyl knight,   *Forth then went this gentle knight,*
   With a carefull chere;   *With a woeful face;*
   The teris oute of his iyen ran,   *The tears out of his eyes ran,*
   And fell downe by his lere.   *And fell down on his face.*

29 They brought hym to the lodge-dore;   *They brought him to the lodge-door;*
   Whan Robyn hym gan see,   *Where Robin did him see,*
   Full curtesly dyd of his hode   *Full courteously he took off his hood*
   And sette hym on his knee.   *And set him on his knee.*

30 'Welcome, sir knight,' than sayde Robyn   *'Welcome, sir knight,' then said Robin*
   'Welcome arte thou to me;   *'Welcome you are to me;*
   I have **abyde you** fastinge, sir,   *I have awaited you fasting, sir,*
   All these ouris thre.'   *All these hours three.'*

31 Than answered the gentyll knight,   *Then answered the gentle knight,*
   With wordes fayre and fre,   *With words both fair and free,*
   'God the save, goode Robyn,   *'God thee save, good Robin,*
   And all thy fayre meyne.'   *And all thy company.'*

32 They wasshed togeder and wyped bothe,   *They washed together and wiped their hands,*
   And sette **till** theyr dynere;   *And set to their dinner;*
   Brede and wyne they had right ynoughe,   *Bread and wine they had enough,*
   And noumbles of the dere.   *And sweetbreads of the deer.*

33 Swannes and fessauntes they had full gode,   *Swans and pheasants*
   they had full good,
   And foules of the ryvere;   *And fowl from out the river;*
   There fayled none so litell a birde   *Not even the smallest bird they lacked*
   That ever was bred on bryre.   *That ever was bred on briar.*

34 'Do gladly, sir knight,' sayde Robyn;   *'Do gladly, sir knight,' said Robin;*
   'Gramarcy, sir,' sayde he;   *'Thank you, sir,' said he;*
   'Suche a dinere had I nat   *'Such a dinner I have not had*
   Of all these wekys thre.   *For at least weekés three.*

35 'If I come ageyne, Robyn,   *'If I come again, Robin,*
   Here by thys countre,   *Here by this country,*
   As gode a dyner I shall the make   *As good a dinner I shall thee make*
   As **that** thou haest made to me.'   *As you have made for me.'*

36 'Gramarcy, knyght,' sayde Robyn;   *'Thank you, knight,' then said Robin;*
   'My dyner whan **that I have**,   *'My dinner when that I have,*
   I was never so gredy, bi dere worthy God,   *I was never so greedy,*
   by dear worthy God,
   My dyner for to crave.   *My dinner for to crave.*

37 'But pay or ye wende,' sayde Robyn;   *'But pay before you leave,'*
   said Robin;
   'Me thynketh it is gode ryght;   *'I think it only right;*
   It was never the maner, by dere worthi God,   *It was never the custom,*
   by dear worthy God,
   A yoman to pay for a knyhht.'   *A yeomen to pay for a knight.'*

38 'I have nought in my coffers,' saide the knyght,   'I have nought in my coffers,' said the knight,
    'That I may profer for shame.'   That I may proffer for shame':
    'Lytell Johnn, go loke,' sayde **Robyn**,   'Little John, go look,' said Robin,
    'Ne let nat for no blame.   'And do not fear the blame.'

39 'Tel me truth,' than saide Robyn,   'Tell me truth,' than said Robin,
    So God have parte of the.'   'So God have part of thee.'
    I have no more but **ten** shelynges,' sayde the knyght,   'I have only ten shillings,' said the knight,
    So God have parte of me.'   'So God have part of me.'

40 'If thou have no more,' sayde Robyn,   'If thou have no more,' said Robin,
    I woll nat one peny;   'I will not take one penny;
    And yf thou had nede of any more,   And if thou had need of any more,
    More shall I lend the.'   More shall I lend thee.'

41 'Go nowe furth, Littell Johnn,   'Go now forth, Little John,
    The truth tell thou me;   The truth tell thou me;
    If there be no more but ten shelinges,   If there be no more but ten shillings,
    Not one peny that I se.'   Not one penny will I see.'

42 Lytell Johnn sprede downe hys mantell   Little John spread out his mantle
    Full fayre upon the grounde,   Full fair upon the ground,
    And there he fonde in the knyghtes cofer   And there he found in the knight's coffer
    But even halfe a pounde.   Exactly half a pound.

The Gest of Robyn Hode

43 Littell Johnn let it lye full styll, / Little John let it lie full still,
And went to hys maysteer full lowe; / And went to his master beloved;
'What **tydynge**, Johnn?' sayde Robyn; / 'What tidings, John?' said Robin;
'Sir, the knyght is true inowe.' / 'Sir, the knight is true enough.'

44 'Fyll of the best wine,' sayde Robyn, / 'A glass of the best wine!' said Robin,
'The knyght shall begynne; / 'The knight shall begin;
Moche wonder thinketh me / A great wonder it seems to me
Thy clothynge is so thinne. / Thy clothing is so thin.'

45 'Tell me one worde,' sayde Robyn, / 'Tell me one word,' said Robin,
'And counsel shal it be; / 'Explain it, if you please;
I trowe thou werte made a knyght of force / I think you were made a knight by force
Or ellys of yemanry. / Or else of yeomanry.

46 'Or ellys thou hast bene a sori husbande, / 'Or else you have been a sorry husband,
And lyved in stroke and stryfe; / And lived in quarrel and strife;
An okerer, or ellis a lechoure,' sayde Robyn, / An usurer, or else a lecher,' said Robin,
'Wyth wronge hast led thy lyfe.' / 'With wrong hast led thy life.'

47 'I am none of those,' sayde the knyght, / 'I am none of those,' said the knight,
'By God that made me; / 'By God that made me;
An hundred wynter here before / An hundred winter here before
Myn ancestres knyghtes have be. / Mine ancestors knights have been.

48 'But oft it hath befal, Robyn,
   A man hath be disgrate;
   But God that sitteth in heven above
   May amende his state.

49 'Withyn this two yere, Robyne,' he said,

   My neghbours well it **knowe**,
   Foure hundred pounde of gode money

   Ful well that myght I **spende**.

50 'Nowe have I no gode,' saide the knyght,

   'God hath shapen such an ende,
   But my chyldren and my wyfe,
   Tyll God yt may **amende.'**

51 'In what maner,' sayde Robyn,
   'Hast thou lorne thy rychesse?'
   'For my greate foly,' he sayde,
   'And for my kyndenesse.

52 'I hade a sone, forsoth, Robyn,
   That shulde have ben myn ayre,
   Whanne he was twenty wynter olde,
   In felde wolde just full fayre.

'But oft it hath befall, Robin,
A man hath be disgraced;
But God that sits in heaven above
May amend his state.

'Within this two years,
Robin,' he said,
My neighbors well it ken,
Four hundred pounds
of good money
Full well that might I spend.

'Now have I no good,'
said the knight,
'God hath shapéd such an end,
But my children and my wife,
Till God it may amend.'

'In what manner,' said Robin,
Hast thou lost thy riches?'
For my great folly,' he said,
And for my kindness.

'I had a son, forsooth, Robin,
That should have been mine heir,
When he was twenty winters old,
In field would joust full fair.

The Gest of Robyn Hode

53 'He slewe a knyght of **Lancastshyre**,*   *'He slew a knight of Lancashire,*
    And a squyer bolde;   *And a squire bold;*
    For to save him in his ryght   *For to save him in his plight*
    My godes both **sette** and solde.   *My goods both pledged and sold.*

54 'My londes both sette to wedde, Robyn,   *'My lands all pledged away, Robin,*
    Untyll a certayn day,   *Until a certain day,*
    To a ryche abbot here besyde   *To a rich abbot here beside*
    Of Seynt Mari Abbey.'   *Of Saint Mary's Abbey.'*

55 'What is the som?' sayde Robyn;   *'What is the sum?' said Robin;*
    'Trouth than tell thou me;'   *'Truth then tell thou me.'*
    'Sir,' he sayde, 'foure hundred pounde;   *'Sir,' he said, 'four hundred pounds;*
    The abbot told it to me.'   *The abbot told it to me.'*

56 'Nowe and thou lese thy lond,' sayde Robyn,   *'Now if thou lose thy land,' said Robin,*
    'What shall fall of the?'   *What shall become of thee?'*
    'Hastely I wol me buske,' sayd the knyght,   *'Hastily I will set out,' said the knight,*
    'Over the salte see.   *Over the salty sea.*

57 'And se where Criste was quyke and dede,   *'And see where Christ was alive and died,*
    On the mount of Calvere;   *On the mount of Calvary;*
    Farewel, frende, and have gode day;   *Farewell, friend, and have good day;*
    It may **not** better be.'   *It may not better be.'*

58 Teris fell out of hys iyen two;
He wolde have gone hys way:
'Farewel, frende, and have gode day;

I ne have no more to pay.'

59 'Where be thy frendes,' sayde Robyn.

'Syr, never one wol me knowe;
While I was ryche ynowe at home
Great boste than wolde they blowe.

60 'And now they renne away fro me,
As bestis on a rowe;
They take no more hede of me
Thanne they had me never sawe.'

61 For ruthe thanne wept Litell Johnn
Scathelock and Much also in fere.
'Fyl of the best wyne,' sayde Robyn,
'For here is a symple chere.

62 **'Hast thou any frendes,' sayde Robyn,**

'Thy borowes that wyll be?'
'I have none,' than sayde the knyght,
'But God that dyed on a tree.'

Tears fell out of his eyes two;
He would have gone his way:
'Farewell, friend,
and have good day;
I have no more to pay.'

'Where are thy friends?'
said Robin.

'Sir, never one will me know;
While I was rich enough at home
Great boast then would they blow!

'And now they run away from me,
As beasts in a row;
They take no more heed of me
Than they had me never saw.'

For sorrow then wept Little John
Scathelock and Much as a pair;
'Fill of the best wine,' said Robin,
For here is a simple cheer.'

'Hast thou any friends,'
said Robin,
Thy guarantors that will be?'
'I have none,' then said the knight,
But God that died on a tree.'

The Gest of Robyn Hode

63 'Do away thy japis,' than sayde Robyn,   'Do away thy jokes,' than said Robin,

   'Thereof wol I right none;   'Guarantor that is none;
   Wenest thou I **will** have God to borowe,   Thinkest thou I will have God to lend,

   Peter, Poule, or Johnn?'   Peter, Paul, or John?'

64 'Nay, by hym that me made,   'Nay, by him that me made,
   And shope both sonne and mone,   And shaped both sun and moon,
   Fynde **me** a better borowe,' sayde Robyn,   Find me a better guarantor,' said Robin,

   'Or money getest thou none.'   Or money getest thou none.'

65 'I have none other,' sayde the knyght,   'I have none other,' said the knight,
   'The sothe for to say,   'The truth for to say,
   But yf yt be Our dere Lady;   But that it be our dear Lady;
   She fayled me never or thys day.'   She failed me never to this day.'

66 'By dere worthy God,' sayde Robyn,   'By dear worthy God,' said Robin,
   'To seche all Englonde thorowe,   You may search all England 'round,
   Yet fonde I never to my pay   Yet found I never to my pay
   A moche better borowe.   A better guarantee for a loan.

67 'Come nowe furth, Litell Johnn   'Come now forth, Little John
   And go to my tresoure,   And go to my treasury,
   And bringe me foure hundered pound,   And bring me four hundred pound,

   And loke well tolde it be.'   And see that well-counted it be.'

68 Furth than went Litell Johnn
    And **Scathelock** went before;
    He tolde oute foure hundred pounde
    By **eightene-and-two score.**

Forth then went Little John
And Scathelock went before;
He counted out four hundred pound
By eighteen and two score.

69 'Is thys well tolde?' sayde **litell** Much;

    Johnn sayde, 'What greveth the?
    It is almus to helpe a gentyll knyght,
    That is fal in poverte.

'Is this well-counted?'
said little Much;
John said, 'What bothers thee?
It is alms to help a gentle knight,
That is fallen in poverty.

70 'Master,' than sayde Lityll Johnn
    'His clothinge is full thynne;
    Ye must gyve the knight a lyveray
    To **helpe** his body therin.

'Master,' then said Little John
'His clothing is full thin;
You must give the knight a livery
To help his body therein.

71 'For ye have scarlet and grene, mayster,

    And many a riche aray;
    There is no marchaunt in mery Englond

    So ryche, I dare well say.'

'For you have scarlet
and green, master,
And many a rich array;
There is no merchant
in merry England
So rich, I dare well say.'

72 'Take hym thre yerdes of every colour,

    And loke well mete that it be.'
    Lytell Johnn toke none other mesure
    But his bowe-tree.

'Take him three yards
of every color,
And look well measured that it be.'
Little John took no other measure
But the length of his bow-tree.

The Gest of Robyn Hode

73 And **of** every handfull that he met / He leped footes three; / 'What devylles drapar,' sayid litell Muche, / 'Thynkest thou for to be?'

And of every handful that he took / He lept another feet three; / 'What devil's draper,' said little Much, / Thinkest thou for to be?'

74 **Scathelock** stode full stil and loughe, / And sayd, 'By God Almyght, / Johnn may gyve hym gode mesure, / **For it costeth hym but** lyght.'

Scathelock stood full still and laughed, / And said, 'By God Almight, / John may give him good measure, / For it costeth him but light.'

75 'Mayster,' than said Litell Johnn / **To gentill** Robyn Hode, / 'Ye must give the knight an hors, / To lede home all this gode.'

'Master,' then said Little John / To gentle Robin Hood, / 'Ye must give the knight an horse, / To lead home all his goods.'

76 'Take hym a gray coursar,' sayde Robyn, / 'And a saydle newe; / He is Oure Ladye's messangere; / God **leve*** that he be true.'

'Give him a gray courser,' said Robin, / And a saddle new; / He is Our Lady's messenger; / God grant that he be true.'

77 'And a gode palfray,' sayde lytell Much, / 'To mayntene hym in his right;' / 'And a peyre of botes,' sayde Scathelock, / 'For he is a gentyll knight.'

'And a good palfrey,' said Little Much, / To maintain him in his right.' / 'And a pair of boots,' said Scathelock, / 'For he is a gentle knight.'

78 'What shalt thou gyve him, Litell John?' said Robyn

    'Sir, a peyre of gilt sporis **clere**,
    To pray for all this company;
    God bringe hym oute of tene.'

79 'Whan shal mi day be,' said the knight,

    'Sir, and your wyll be?'
    'This day twelve moneth,' saide Robyn,

    'Under this grene-wode tre.

80 'It were greate shame,' sayde Robyn,
    'A knight alone to ryde,
    Withoute squyre, yoman, or page,
    To walke by his syde.

81 'I shall the lende Litell John, my man,

    For he shalbe thy knave,
    In a yeman's stede he may the stande

    If thou greate nede have.

What shalt thou give him, Little John?' said Robin
Sir, a pair of gilt spurs set,
To pray for all this company;
God bring him out of debt.'

'When shall my day be?' said the knight,
Sir, if your will it be?'
'This day twelve month,' said Robin,
Under this greenwood tree.

'It were great shame,' said Robin,
A knight alone to ride,
Without squire, yeoman, or page,
To walk by his side.

'I shall thee lend Little John, my man,
For he shall be thy knave,
In a yeoman's stede he may thee stand
If thou great need have.'

The Gest of Robyn Hode

The Seconde Fytte   The Second Fit

82 Now is the knight gone on his way;
    This game hym thought full gode;
    Whanne he loked on Bernesdale
    He blessyd Robyn Hode.

Now is the knight gone on his way;
This game he thought full good;
When he looked on Barnsdale
He blesséd Robin Hood.

83 And whanne he thought on Bernysdale,
    On **Scathelock**, Much, and Johnn,
    He blyssyd them for the best company
    That ever he in come.

And when he thought on Barnsdale,
On Scathelock, Much, and John,
He blessed them for the best company
That ever he in come.

84 Then spake that gentyll knyght
    To Lytel Johan gan he saye,
    'To-morrowe I must to Yorke toune,
    To Saynt Mary abbay.

Then spoke that gentle knight
To Little John he did say,
Tomorrow I must to York town,
To Saint Mary's Abbey.

85 'And to the abbot of that place
    Foure hondred pounde I must pay;
    And but I be there upon this nyght
    My londe is lost for ay.'

And to the abbot of that place
Four hundred pound I must pay;
Unless I be there upon this night
My land is lost for aye.

86 The abbot sayd to his covent,
    There he stode on grounde,
    'This day twelfe moneth came there a knyght
    And borowed foure hundred pounde.

The abbot said to his convent,
There he stood on ground,
'This day twelve month came there a knight
And borrowed [many a] pound.

87 ....*   ['He borrowed full four hundred pound]
   Upon all his londe fre;   Upon all his land free;
   But he come this ylke day   Unless he come this very day
   Dysheryte shall he be.'   Disherited shall he be.'

88 'It is full erely,' sayd the pryoure,   'It is still early,' said the prior,
   'The day is not yet ferre gone;   'The day is not yet far gone;
   I had lever to pay an hondrede pounde, [Before the knight disherited be,
   And lay downe anone.   An hundred pounds I'd lay down.]

89 'The knyght is ferre beyonde the see,   'The knight is far beyond the sea,
   In Englonde **he is*** ryght,   He [cannot guard his English] rights,
   And suffreth honger and colde,   And suffers hunger and cold,
   And many a sory nyght.   And many a sorry night.

90 'It were grete pyte,' said the pryoure,   'It were great pity,' said the prior,
   'So to have his londe;   So to have his land;
   And ye be so lyght of your consyence,   And ye be so light
                                                    of your conscience,
   Ye do to hym moch wronge.'   Ye do to him much wrong.'

91 'Thou arte ever in my berde,' sayd the abbot, 'Thou art ever in my
                                                       beard,' said the abbot,
   'By God and Saynt **Rycharde**.'   'By God and Saint Richard.'
   With that cam in a fat-heded monke,   With that came in a
                                                       fat-headed monk,
   The heygh selerer.   The high cellarer.

The Gest of Robyn Hode

92 'He is dede or hanged,' sayd the monke,   *'He is dead or hanged,' said the monk,*

'By God that bought me dere,   *'By God that bought me dear,*
And we shall have to spende in this place   *And we shall have to spend in this place*

Foure hundred pounde by yere.'   *Four hundred pounds each year.'*

93 The abbot and the hy selerer   *The abbot and the high cellarer*
    Sterte forthe full bolde,   *Started forth full bold,*
    The **justyce*** of Englonde   *The Justice of England*
    The abbot there dyde holde.   *The abbot there did hold.*

94 The hye justyce and many mo   *The High Justice and many more*
    Had take in to they honde   *Had taken their pay so long,*
    Holy all the knyghtes det,   *Guarding all the knight's debt*
    To put that knyght to wronge.   *To put that knight to wrong.*

95 They demed the knyght wonder sore,   *They deemed the knight very poor,*
    The abbot and his meyne: *The abbot's company:*
    'But he come this ylke day   *'Unless he come this very day*
    Dysheryte shall he be.'   *Disherited shall he be.'*

96 'He wyll not come yet,' sayd the justyce,   *'He will not come yet,' said the Justice,*

'I dare well undertake.'   *'I dare well undertake.'*
But in sorowe tyme for them all   *But at a sorrowful time for them all*
The knyght came to the gate.   *The knight came to the gate.*

97 Than bespake that gentyll knyght
    Untyll his meyne,
    'Now put on your symple wedes
    That ye brought fro the see.

*Then bespoke that gentle knight
Unto his company,
'Now put on your simple clothes
That ye brought from the sea.'*

98 ....*
    They came to the gates anone;
    The porter was redy hymselfe,
    And welcomed them everychone.

*[So they put on their poor clothes;]
They came to the gates anon;
The porter was ready himself,
And welcomed them everyone.*

99 'Welcome, syr knyght,' sayd the porter;

    'My lorde to mete is he,
    And so is many a gentyll man,
    For the love of the.'

*'Welcome, sir knight,'
said the porter;
My lorde at dinner is he,
And so is many a gentle man,
For the love of thee.'*

100 The porter swore a full grete othe,
    'By God that made me,
    Here is the best coresed hors
    That ever yet sawe I me.

*The porter swore a full grete oath,
By God that made me,
'Here is the very handsomest horse
That ever yet saw I me.'*

101 'Lede them in to the stable,' he sayd,
    'That eased myght they be.'
    'They shall not come therin,' sayd the knyght,

    'By God that dyed on a tre.'

*'Lead them into the stable,' he said,
'That eased might they be.'
'They shall not
come therein,' said the knight,
'By God that died on a tree.'*

The Gest of Robyn Hode

102 Lordes were to mete isette
    In that abbotes hall;
    The knyght went forth and kneled downe
    And salued them grete and small.

Lords were to dinner met / In that abbot's hall; / The knight went forth and kneeled down / And greeted them great and small.

103 'Do gladly, syr abbot,' sayd the knyght,
    'I am come to holde my day:'
    The fyrst word the abbot spake,
    'Hast thou brought my pay?'

'Do gladly, sir abbot,' said the knight, / 'I am come to hold my day:' / The first word the abbot spoke, / 'Has thou brought my pay?'

104 'Not one peny,' sayd the knyght,
    'By God that maked me.'
    'Thou art a shrewed dettour,' sayd the abbot;
    'Syr justyce, drynke to me.'

'Not one penny,' said the knight, / 'By God that makéd me.' / 'Thou art a shrewd debtor,' said the abbot; / 'Sir Justice, drink to me.'

105 'What doost thou here,' sayd the abbot,
    'But thou haddest brought thy pay?'
    'For God,' than sayd the knyght,
    'To pray of a lenger daye.'

'What dost thou here,' said the abbot, / 'If you have not brought thy pay?' / ''Fore God,' then said the knight, / 'To pray for a longer day.'

106 'Thy daye is broke,' sayd the justyce,
    'Londe getest thou none.'
    'Now, good syr justyce, be my frende,
    And fende me of my fone!'

'Thy day is broke,' said the Justice, / 'Land getest thou none.' / 'Now, good sir Justice, be my friend, / And guard me from my foes!'

107 'I am holde with the abbot,' sayd the justyce,

    'Both with cloth and fee.'
    'Now, good syr sheryf, be my frende!'

    'Nay, for God,' sayd he.

108 'Now, good syr abbot, be my frende,
    For thy curteyse,
    And holde my londes in thy honde
    Tyll I have made the gree!

109 'And I wyll be thy true servaunte,
    And trewely serve the,
    Tyl ye have foure hondrede pounde
    Of money good and free.'

110 The abbot sware a full grete othe,
    'By God that dyed on a tree,
    Get the londe where thou may,
    For thou getest none of me.'

111 'By dere worthy God,' then sayd the knyght,

    'That all this worlde wrought,
    'But I have my londe agayne,
    'Full dere it shall be bought.'

'I am bound to the abbot,' said the Justice,
    Both with cloth and fee:'
    'Now, good sir sheriff, be my friend!'
    'Nay, 'fore God,' said he.

'Now, good sir abbot, be my friend,
    For thy courtesy,
    And hold my lands in thy hand
    Till I have paid the fee!

'And I will be thy true servant,
    And truly serve thee,
    Till ye have four hundred pounds
    Of money good and free.'

The abbot swore a full great oath
    By God that dyed on a tree,
    'Get thee land where thou may,
    For thou getest none of me.'

'By dear worthy God,' then said the knight,
    'That all this world wrought,
    Unless I have my land again,
    Full dear it shall be bought.'

112 God, that was of a mayden borne,   *God, that was of a maiden born,*
    Leve us well to spede!   *Grant us well to speed!*
    For it is good to assay a frende   *For it is good to assay a friend*
    Or that a man have nede.   *Before a man have need.*

113 The abbot lothely on hym gan loke, *The abbot loathingly on him did look,*
    And vylaynesly hym gan **call**;   *And a churl he did him call;*
    'Out,' he sayd, 'thou false knyght,   *'Out,' he said, 'thou false knight,*
    Spede the out of my hall!'   *Speed thee out of my hall!'*

114 'Thou lyest,' then sayd the gentyll knyght,   *'Thou liest,' then said the gentle knight,*
    'Abbot, in thy hal;   *'Abbot, in thy hall;*
    False knyght was I never,   *False knight was I never,*
    By God that made us all.'   *By God that made us all.'*

115 Up then stode that gentyll knyght,   *Up then stood that gentle knight;*
    To the abbot sayd he,   *To the abbot said he,*
    'To suffre a knyght to knele so longe,   *'To suffer a knight to kneel so long,*
    Thou canst no curteysye.   *Thou knowest no courtesy.*

116 'In joustes and in tournement   *'In jousts and in tournament*
    Full ferre than have I be,   *Full far then have I been,*
    And put my selfe as ferre in prees   *And put myself as far in the press*
    As ony that ever I se.   *As any that I have seen.'*

117 'What wyll ye gyve more,' sayd the justice,   *'What will ye give more,'*
said the Justice,

    'And the knyght shall make a releyse?   *'If the knight shall*
make a release?

    And elles dare I safly swere   *Otherwise dare I safely swear*
    Ye holde never your londe in pees.'   *Ye will never hold*
your land in peace.'

118 'An hondred pounde,' sayd the abbot;   *'An hundred pound,'*
said the abbot;

    The justice sayd, 'Gyve hym two.'   *The Justice said, 'Give him two.'*
    'Nay, be God,' sayd the knyght,   *'Nay, by God,' said the knight,*
    'Yit gete ye it not so.   *'Yet get ye it not so.*

119 'Though ye wolde gyve a thousand more,   *'Though you would give*
a thousand more,

    Yet were **ye** never the nere;   *Yet were ye never the nearer;*
    Shall there never be myn heyre   *Shall there never be mine heir*
    Abbot, justice, ne frere.'   *Abbot, justice, nor friar.'*

120 He stert hym to a borde anone,   *He unto a board at once,*
    Tyll a table rounde,   *To a table round,*
    And there he shoke oute of a bagge   *And there he shook out of a bag*
    Even four hundred pound.   *Even four hundred pound.*

121 'Have here thi golde, sir abbot,' saide the knight,   'Have here thy gold, sir abbot,' said the knight,
    'Which that thou lentest me;   'Which that thou lent to me;
    Had thou ben curtes at my comynge,   Had thou been courteous at my coming,
    Rewarded shouldest thou have be.'   Rewarded shouldest thou have been.'

122 The abbot sat styll, and ete no more,   The abbot sat still, and ate no more,
    For all his ryall fare;   For all his royal fare;
    He cast his hede on his shulder,   He cast his head on his shoulder,
    And fast began to stare.   And fast began to stare.

123 'Take me my golde agayne,' said the abbot,   'Give me my gold again,' said the abbot,
    'Sir justice, that I toke the.'   Sir Justice, that I gave thee:'
    'Not a peni,' said the justice,   'Not a penny,' said the Justice,
    'Bi God that dyed on tree.'   By God that died on tree.'

124 'Sir abbot, and ye men of lawe,   'Sir abbot, and ye men of law,
    Now have I holde my daye;   Now have I held my day;
    Now shall I have my londe agayne,   Now shall I have my land again,
    For ought that you can saye.'   For ought that you can say.'

125 The knyght stert out of the dore,   The knight started out of the door,
    Awaye was all his care,   Gone was all his care,
    And on he put his good clothynge,   And on he put his good clothing,
    The other he lefte there.   The other he left there.

126 He wente hym forth full mery syngynge, *He went forth singing merrily,*
  As men have tolde in tale; *As men have told in tale;*
  His lady met hym at the gate, *His lady met him at the gate,*
  At home in **Verysdale**.* *At home in Verysdale.*

127 'Welcome, my lorde,' sayd his lady; *'Welcome, my lord,' said his lady;*
  'Syr, lost is all your good?' *Sir, lost is all your good?'*
  'Be mery, dame,' sayd the knyght, *'Be merry, dame,' said the knight,*
  'And pray for Robyn Hode. *'And pray for Robin Hood.*

128 'That ever his soule be in blysse; *'That ever his soul be in bliss;*
  He holpe me out of tene; *He helped me out of debt;*
  Ne had **not be** his kyndenesse, *Had it not been for his kindness,*
  Beggars had we bene. *Beggars we were set.*

129 'The abbot and I accorded ben, *'The abbot and I accorded have been,*
  He is served of his pay; *He is served of his pay;*
  The god yoman lent it me, *The good yeoman lent it me,*
  As I cam by the way.' *As I came by the way.'*

130 This knight than dwelled fayre at home, *This knight then dwelléd fair at home,*
  The sothe for to saye, *The truth for to say,*
  Tyll he had gete four hundred pound, *Till he had got four hundred pound,*
  Al redy for to pay. *All ready for to pay.*

The Gest of Robyn Hode

131 He purveyed him an hundred bowes	He purveyed him an hundred bowes
The strynges well ydyght,	The strings well-made to fight,
An hundred shefe of arowes gode,	An hundred sheafs of arrows good,
The hedys burneshed full bryght;	The heads burnished full bright;
132 And every arowe an elle longe,	And every arrow an ell long,
With pecok well idyght,	With peacock feathers for flights,
Inocked all with whyte silver;	Marked all with white silver;
It was a semely syght.	It was a lovely sight.
133 He purveyed hym an hundreth men	He purveyed him an hundred men
Well harnessed in that stede,	Well harnessed as he led
And hym selfe in that same sete,	And himself in that same seat,
And clothed in whyte and rede.	And clothed in white and red.
134 He bare a launsgay in his honde,	He bore a light lance in his hand;
And a man ledde his male,	A man led his cart of mail,
And reden with a lyght songe	He rode with a light song
Unto Bernysdale.	Unto Barnsdale.
135 **But as he went at a brydge**	But as he came to a bridge
Ther was a wrastelyng,*	There was a wrestling,
....*	[With many men gathering there]
....*	[To win the garland of spring.]
135A ...*.	[And many fought to win the prize,]
And there taryed was he,	And there delayed was he,
And there was all the best yemen	And there were all the best yeomen
Of all the west countree.	Of all the west country.

136 A full fayre game there was up set,   A full fair game there was up set,
      A whyte bulle up i-pyght,   A white bull the prize for the fight,
      A grete courser, with sadle and brydil,   A great courser,
                                                               with saddle and bridle,
    With golde burnyssht full bryght.   With gold burnished full bright.

137 A payre of gloves, a rede golde rynge,   A pair of gloves, a red gold ring,
      A pype of wyne, in **good** fay;   A pipe of wine, in good fay;
      What man that bereth hym best i-wys   What man that
                                                              performed the best, I say,
    The pryce shall bere away.   The price should bear away.

138 There was a yoman in that place,   There was a yeoman in that place,
      And best worthy was he,   And best worthy was he,
      And for he was ferre and frembde bested,   And since he was
                                                               far from his home,
    Slayne he shulde have be.   Slain he should have been.

139 The knight had ruthe of this yoman,   The knight had news
                                                              of this yeoman,
      In place **where that** he stode;   In place where that he stood;
      He sayde that yoman shulde have no harme,   He said that yeoman
                                                            should have no harm,
    For love of Robyn Hode.   For love of Robin Hood.

140 The knyght presed in to the place,   The knight pressed into the place,
      An hundreth folowed hym **free**   An hundred followed him free
      With bowes bent and arowes sharpe,   With bows bent and arrows sharp,
      For to shende that companye.   For to halt that company.

The Gest of Robyn Hode

141 They shulderd all and made hym rome,　　　*They pushed aside and made him room*

　　To wete what he wolde say;　　　　　*To learn what he would say;*
　　He toke the yeman bi the hande,　　　*He took the yeoman by the hand,*
　　And gave hym al the play.　　　　　　*And gave him all the play.*

142 He gave him fyve marke for his wyne,　　*He gave him five marks for his win,*

　　There it lay on the molde,　　　　　　*There it lay on the mold,*
　　And bad it shulde be set a broche,　　*And bade a cask of wine be broached,*
　　Drynke who so wolde.　　　　　　　　　*Drink it who so would.*

143 Thus longe taried this gentyll knyght,　*Thus long tarried this gentle knight,*

　　Tyll that play was done;　　　　　　　*Till that play was done;*
　　So longe abode Robyn fastinge,　　　　*So long abode Robin fasting,*
　　Thre houres after the none.　　　　　 *Three hours after the noon.*

The Thirde Fytte　　　　　　　　　　　### The Third Fit

144 Lyth and lystyn, gentilmen,　　　　　　*Stop and listen, gentlemen,*
　　All that nowe be here;　　　　　　　　*All that now be here;*
　　Of Litell Johnn, that was the knightes man,　*Of Little John, that was the knight's man,*

　　Goode myrth ye shall here.　　　　　　*Goode mirth ye shall hear.*

145 It was upon a mery day　　　　　　　　*It was upon a merry day*
　　That yonge men wolde go shete;　　　　*That young men would go shoot;*
　　Lytell Johnn fet his bowe anone,　　　*Little John fetched his bow anon,*
　　And sayde he wolde them mete.　　　　*And said he would them meet.*

The Gest of Robyn Hode

146 Thre tymes Litell Johnn shet aboute,   *Three times Little John shot about,*
　　And alwey he **slet** the wande;   *And always he slit the wand;*
　　The proude sherif of Notingham   *The proud sheriff of Nottingham*
　　By the markes can stande.   *By the marks he did stand.*

147 The sherif swore a full greate othe: *The sheriff swore a full great oath,*
　　'By hym that dyede on a tre,   *'By him that died on a tree,*
　　This man is the best arschere   *This man is the best archer*
　　That ever yet **sawe I me**.   *That ever yet saw I me.*

148 'Say me nowe, wight yonge man,   *Tell me now, strong young man,*
　　What is nowe thy name?   *What is now thy name?*
　　In what countre were thou borne,   *In what country were thou born,*
　　And where is thy wonynge wane?'   *And [how you so skilled became]?'*

149 In Holdernes, sir, I was borne,   *'In Holderness, sir, I was born,*
　　I-wys al of my dame;   *And came forth from my dame;*
　　Men cal me Reynolde Grenelef   *Men call me Reynold Greenleaf*
　　Whan I am at home.'   *When I am at home.'*

150 'Sey me, Reynolde Grenelefe,   *'Tell me, Reynold Greenleaf,*
　　Wolde thou dwell with me?   *Would thou dwell with me?*
　　And every yere I woll the gyve   *And every year I will the give*
　　Twenty marke to thy fee.'   *Twenty marks to thy fee.'*

151 'I have a maister,' sayde Litell Johnn   *'I have a master,' said Little John*
　　'A curteys knight is he;   *'A courteous knight is he;*
　　May ye leve get of hym,   *If ye get leave of him,*
　　The better may it be.'   *The better may it be.'*

The Gest of Robyn Hode

152 The sherif gate Litell John
    Twelve monethes of the knight;
    Therfore he gave him right anone
    A gode hors and a wight.

The sheriff got Little John
*   Twelve months of the knight;*
*   Therefore he gave him right away*
*   A good horse of great might.*

153 Nowe is Litell John the sherifes man,

    God lende us well to spede!
    But alwey thought Lytell John
    To quyte him wele his mede.

Now Little John is
*   the sheriff's man,*
God grant us well to speed!
But always thought Little John
To to requite him for his deeds.

154 'Nowe so God me helpe,' sayde Litell John,

    'And by my true leutye,
    I shall be the worst servaunt to hym
    That ever yet had he.'

'Now so God me help,'
*   said Little John,*
And by my true loyalty,
I shall be the worst servant to him
That ever yet had he.'

155 It **befell** upon a Wednesday
    The sherif on huntynge was gone,
    And Litel John lay in his bed,
    And was foriete at home.

It befell upon a Wednesday
*   The sherif a-hunting was gone,*
*   And Little John lay in his bed,*
*   And was forgotten at home.*

156 Therfore he was fastinge
    Til it was past the none;
    'Gode sir stuarde, I pray to the,
    Gyve **me to dine**,' saide Litell John.

Therefore he was fasting
*   Till it was past the noon;*
*   'Good sir steward, I pray to thee,*
*   Gyve me to dine,' said Little John.*

157 'It is longe for Grenelefe / 'It is longe for Greenleaf
    Fastinge thus for to be; / Fasting thus for to be;
    Therfore I pray the, sir stuarde, / Therefore I pray thee, sir steward,
    Mi dyner **gyve thou** me.' / My dinner give thou me.'

158 'Shalt thou never ete ne drynke,' saide the stuarde, / 'Shalt thou never eat nor drink,' said the steward,
    'Tyll my lorde be come to towne:' / 'Till my lord be come to town:'
    'I make myn avowe to God,' saide Litell John, / I make mine avowe to God,' said Little John,
    'I have lever to crake thy crowne.' / 'I have sooner to crack thy crown.'

159 The boteler was full uncurteys, / The butler was full uncourteous,
    There he stode on flore; / There he stood on floor;
    He start to the botery / He start to the buttery
    And shet fast the dore. / And shut fast the door.

160 Lytell Johnn gave the boteler suche a **tap** / Little John gave the butler such a tap
    His backe **yede nigh in two;** / His back broke nigh in two;
    Though he lived an hundred **wynter,** / Though he lived an hundred winter,
    The wors shuld he go. / The worse should he go.

161 He sporned the dore with his fote; / He spurned the door with his foot;
    It went open wel and fyne; / It went open well and fine;
    And there he made large lyveray, / And there he made great liberty,
    Bothe of ale and of wyne. / Both of ale and of wine.

162 'Sith ye wol nat dyne,' sayde Litell John

    'I shall gyve you to drinke;
    And though ye lyve an hundred wynter

    On Lytel Johnn ye shall thinke.'

163 Litell John ete, and Litel John drank,

    The while that he wolde;
    The sherife had in his kechyne a coke,

    A stoute man and a bolde.

164 'I make myn avowe to God,' saide the coke,

    'Thou arte a shrewde **hynde**
    In **any hous for** to dwel,
    For to aske thus to dyne.'

165 And there he lent Litell John
    Gode strokis thre;
    'I make myn **avowe**,' sayde Lytell John,

    'These strokis lyked well me.'

'Since ye will not dine,'
said Little John,
I shall give you to drink;
And though ye live
an hundred winter
On Little John you shall think.'

Little John ate, and
Little John drank,
The while that he would;
The sheriff had in his
kitchen a cook,
A stout man and a bold.

'I make mine avowe
to God,' said the cook,
Thou arte a shrewd hind
In any house for to dwell,
For to ask thus to dine.'

And there he lent Little John
Good strokés three;
'I make mine avowe,'
said Little John,
'These strokés liked well me.'

166 'Thou arte a bolde man and an hardy,   'Thou arte a bold man and an hardy,

    And so thinketh me;   And so thinketh me;
    And or I pas fro this place   And ere I pass from this place
    Asseyed better shalt thou be.'   Assayed better shalt thou be.'

167 Lytell Johnn drew a ful gode sworde,   Little John drew a full good sword,
    The coke toke another in hande;   The cook took another in hand;
    They thought no thynge for to fle,   They never thought to flee,
    But stifly for to stande.   But stiffly for to stand.

168 There they faught sore togedere   There they fought sore together
    Two myle way and well more;   For [half an hour] and more;
    Myght neyther other harme done   Neither could do the other harm
    The mountnaunce of an owre.   The full length of an hour.

169 'I make myn avowe to God,' saye Litell Johnn,   'I make mine avowe to God,' said Little John,

    'And by my true lewte,   'And by my true loyalty,
    Thou are one of the best sworde-men   Thou are one of the best swordsmen

    That ever yit **sawe I me.**   That ever yet saw I me.

The Gest of Robyn Hode

170 'Cowdest thou shote as well in a bowe,

    To grene wode thou shuldest with me,

    And two times in the yere thy clothinge

    I-chaunged shulde be.

171 'And every yere of Robyn Hode
    Twenty merke to thy fe:'
    'Put up thy swerde,' saide the coke,
    'And felowees woll we be.'

172 Then he fet to Lytell Johnn
    The nowmbles of a do,
    Gode brede, and full gode wyne;
    They ete and drank theretoo.

173 And when they had dronkyn well,
    Theyre trouthes togeder they plight
    That they wolde be with Robyn
    That ylke same nyght.

174 They dyd them to the tresoure-hows,

    As fast as they myght gone;
    The lokkes, that were of full gode stele,

    They brake them everichone.

*'Couldst thou shoot
as well with a bow,
To greenwood thou
shouldest with me,
And two times in
the year thy clothing
Changéd it should be.*

*'And every year of Robin Hood
Twenty marks to thy fee.'
'Put up thy sword,' said the cook,
'And fellows will we be.'*

*Then he fed to Little John
The sweetmeats of a doe,
Good bread, and full good wine;
They ate and drank thereto.*

*And when they had drunken well,
Their troths together they plight
That they would be with Robin
That very same night.*

*They did them to
the treasure-house,
As fast as they might gone;
The locks, that were of
full good steel,
They broke them every one.*

175 They toke away the silver vessell,   *They took away the silver vessels,*
      And all that thei might get;   *And all that they might get;*
      Pecis, masars, ne sponis,   *Dishes, cups, nor spoons,*
      Wolde **they none** forget.   *Would they not forget.*

176 Also **they** toke the gode pens   *Also they took the good pence,*
      Thre hundred pounde and more,   *Three hundred pounds and more,*
      And did them streyte to Robyn Hode   *And did them straight to Robin Hood*
      Under the grene wode **hore**.   *Under the greenwood hoar.*

177 'God the save, my dere mayster,   *'God thee save, my dear master,*
      And Criste the save and se.'   *And Christ thee save and see.'*
      And thanne sayde Robyn to Litell Johnn,   *And then said Robin to Little John,*
      'Welcome myght thou be.   *'Welcome might thou be.*

178 '**And also** be that fayre yeman   *'And also be that fair yeoman*
      Thou bryngest there with the;   *Thou bringest there with thee;*
      What tydynges fro Notyngham?   *What tidings from Nottingham?*
      Lytill Johnn, tell thou me.'   *Little John, tell thou me.'*

179 'Well the gretith the proude sheryf,   *'Well thee greeteth the proud sheriff,*
      And **sende the** here by me   *And sende thee here by me*
      His coke and his silver vessell,   *His cook and his silver vessels,*
      And thre hundred pounde and thre.'   *And three hundred pounds and three.'*

180 'I make myne avowe to God,' sayde Robyn,   *'I make mine avowe to God,' said Robin,*

    'And to the Trenyte,   *'And to the Trinity,*
    It was never by his gode wyll   *It was never by his good will*
    This gode is come to me.'   *This good is come to me.'*

181 Lytell Johnn **there hym** bethought   *Little John there him bethought*
    On a shrewde wyle;   *On a shrewd wile;*
    Fyve myle in the forest he ran,   *Five miles in the forest he ran,*
    Hym happed all his wyll.   *There happened all his will.*

182 Than he met the proude sheref,   *Then he met the proud sheriff,*
    Huntynge with houndes and horne;   *Hunting with hounds and horn;*
    Lytell Johnn coude of curteyse,   *Little John, who knew his courtesy,*
    And knelyd hym beforne.   *Then kneeled him before.*

183 'God the save, my dere mayster,   *'God thee save, my dear master,*
    And Criste the save and se.'   *And Christ thee save and see.'*
    'Reynolde Grenelefe,' sayde the shryef,   *'Reynold Greenleaf,' said the sheriff,*

    'Where hast thou nowe be?'   *Where now hast thou been?'*

184 'I have be in this forest;   *'I have been in this forest;*
    A fayre syght can I se;   *A fair sight I did see;*
    It was one of the fayrest **syghtes**   *It was one of the fairest sights*
    That ever yet sawe I me.   *That ever yet saw I me.*

185 'Yonder I **se** a ryght fayre harte,   *'Yonder I saw a right fair hart,*
    His coloure is of grene;   *His color is of green;*
    Seven score of dere upon a herde   *Seven score of deer upon a herd*
    Be with hym all bydene.   *With him all remain.*

186 **'Their tyndes*** are so sharpe, maister,   *'Their tines are so sharp, master,*
    Of sexty, and well mo,   *Of sixty, and well more,*
    That I durst not shote for drede   *That I durst not shote for dread*
    Lest they wolde me slo.'   *Lest they would me slew.'*

187 'I make myn avowe to God,' sayde the shyref,   *'I make mine avowe to God,' said the sheriff,*
    'That syght wolde I fayne se.'   *That sight would I fain see.'*
    'Buske you thyderwarde, mi dere mayster,   *'Take you hither, my dear master,*
    Anone, and wende with me.'   *Now, and go with me.'*

188 The sherif rode, and Litell Johnn   *The sheriff rode, and Little John*
    Of fote he was full smerte,   *Of foot he was full smart,*
    And whane they came **afore** Robyn,   *And when they came before Robin,*
    'Lo, sir, here is the mayster herte!'   *'Lo, sir, here is the master hart!'*

189 Still stode the proude sherief,   *Still stood the proud sheriff,*
    A sory man was he;   *A sorry man was he;*
    'Wo the worthe, Raynolde Grenelefe,   *'Woe to thee, Reynold Greenleaf,*
    Thou hast **betrayed nowe** me.'   *Thou hast betrayed now me.'*

The Gest of Robyn Hode

190 'I make myn avowe to God,' sayde Litell Johnn,   *'I make mine avowe*
                                                                                                    to God,' said Little John,
      'Mayster, ye be to blame;   *Master, ye be to blame;*
      I was mysserved of my dynere   *I was mis-served of my dinner*
      Whan I was with you at home.'   *When I was with you at home.'*

191 Sone he was to souper sette,   *Soon he was to supper set,*
      And served **well** with silver white,   *And served well with silver white,*
      And whan the sherif **se** his vessell   *And when the sheriff saw his vessels,*
      For sorowe he myght not ete.   *For sorrow he might not eat.*

192 'Make glad chere,' sayde Robyn Hode,   *'Make glad cheer,'*
                                                                                             said Robin Hood,
      'Sherif, for charite,   *'Sheriff, for charity,*
      And for the love of Litill Johnn   *And for the love of Little John*
      Thy lyfe **is graunted** to the.'   *Thy life is granted to thee.'*

193 Whan they had souped well,   *When they had supped well,*
      The day was al gone;   *The daylight was all gone;*
      Robyn **commande** Litell Johnn   *Robin commande Little John*
      To drawe of his hosen and his shone;   *To draw off his hose and his shoon;*

194 His kirtell, and his cote of pie,   *His kirtle, and his coat of pie,*
      That was fured well and fine,   *That was furred well and fine,*
      And **to** hym a grene mantel,   *And give to him a green mantle,*
      To lap his body therin.   *To wrap his body therein.*

195 Robyn commaundyd his wight yonge men,   *Robin commanded his strong young men,*

    Under the grene-wode tree,   *Under the greenwood tree,*
    They **shall lay** in that same sute,   *They should lay in that same suit,*
    That the sherif myght them see.   *That the sheriff might them see.*

196 All nyght **laye that** proude sherif   *All night lay that proud sheriff*
    In his breche and in his schert;   *In his breeches and in his shirt;*
    No wonder it was, in grene wode,   *No wonder it was, in greenwood,*
    Though his sydes gan to smerte.   *That his sides began to smart.*

197 'Make glade chere,' sayde Robyn Hode,   *'Make glad cheer,' said Robin Hood,*

    'Sheref, for charite;   *Sheriff, for charity;*
    For this is our ordre i-wys,   *For this is our order, I know,*
    Under the grene-wode tree.'   *Under the greenwood tree.'*

198 'This is a harder order,' sayde the sherief,   *'This is a harder order,' said the sheriff,*

    'Than any ankir or frere;   *Than anchorite or friar;*
    For all the golde in mery Englonde   *For all the gold in merry England*
    I wolde nat longe dwell her.'   *I would not longer dwell here.'*

199 'All this twelve monthes,' sayde Robin,   *'All this twelve months,' said Robin,*

    'Thou shalt dwell with me;   *'Thou shalt dwell with me;*
    I shall the teche, proude sherif,   *I shall thee teach, proud sheriff,*
    An outlawe for to be.'   *An outlaw for to be.'*

200 'Or I be here another nyght,' sayde the sherif,   'If I be here another night,' said the sheriff,
'Robyn, nowe **pray I** the,   'Robin, now pray I thee,
Smyte of mijn hede rather to-morowe,   Smite of mine head rather tomorrow,
And I forgyve it the.   And I forgive it thee.'

201 'Lat me go,' than sayde the sherif,   'Let me go,' then said the sheriff,
'For saynte charite,   'For saintly charity,
And I woll be the best frende   And I will be the best friend
That ever yet had ye.'   That ever yet had ye.'

202 'Thou shalt swere me an othe,' sayde Robyn,   'Thou shalt swear me an oath,' said Robin,
'On my bright bronde;   On my bright brand;
Shalt thou never awayte me scathe,   Shalt thou never await me scathe,
By water ne by lande.   By water or by lande.

203 'And if thou fynde any of my men,   'And if thou find any of my men,
By nyght or by day   By night or by day
Upon thyn othe thou shalt swere   Upon thine oath thou shalt swear
To helpe them that thou may.'   To help them that thou may.'

204 Nowe **have** the sherif sworne his othe,   Now has the sheriff sworn his oath,
And home he began to gone;   And home he soon was gone;
He was as full of grene wode   He was as full of greenwood
As ever was hepe of stone.   As ever was rock pile of stone.

The Fourth Fytte / The Fourth Fit

205 The sherif dwelled in Notingham;
    He was fayne he was agone;
    And Robyn and his mery men
    Went to wode anone.

*The sheriff dwelled in Nottingham;
He was fain that he was gone;
And Robin and his merry men
Went to the wood anon.*

206 'Go we to dyner,' sayde Littell Johnn
    Robyn Hode sayde, 'Nay,
    For I drede Our Lady be wroth with me,
    For she sent me nat my pay.'

*'Go we to dinner,' said Little John
Robin Hood said, 'Nay,
For I fear Our Lady be wroth with me,
For she sent me not my pay.'*

207 'Have no doute, maister,' sayde Litell Johnn
    'Yet is nat the sonne at rest;
    For I dare say, and savely swere,
    The knight is true and truste.'

*'Have no doubt, master,' said Little John
'Not yet is the sun at rest;
For I dare say, and safely swear,
The knight you truly can trust.'*

208 'Take thy bowe in thy hande,' sayde Robyn,
    'Late Much wende with the,
    And so shal Wyllyam Scathelock,
    And no man abyde with me.

*'Take thy bow in thy hand,' said Robin,
'Let Much go with thee,
And so shall William Scathelock,
And no man abide with me.*

209 'And walke up under the Sayles,
    And to Watlynge-strete,
    And wayte after such unketh gest;
    Up-chaunce ye may them mete.

*'And walk up under the Saylis,
And to Watling Street
And wait after such unknown guest;
By chance ye may them meet.*

210 'Whether he be messengere,
   Or a man that myrthes can,
   Of my good he shall have some,
   Yf he be a pore man.'

'Whether he be messenger,
Or a man with music in hand,
Of my good he shall have some,
If he be a poor man.'

211 Forth then stert Lytel Johan
   Half in tray and tene,
   And gyrde hym with a full good swerde,
   Under a mantel of grene.

Forth then started Little John
Half in wrath and pain,
And girded him with
a full good sword,
Under a mantle of green.

212 They went up to the Sayles,
   These yeman all thre;
   They loked est, they loked west,
   They myght no man se.

They went up to the Saylis,
These yeoman all three;
They lookéd east, they lookéd west,
They might no man see.

213 But as he loked in Bernysdale
   By the hye waye,
   Than were they ware of two blacke monkes,
   Eche on a good palferay.

But as he looked in Barnsdale
By the high way,
Then they were aware of
two black monks,
Each on a good palfrey.

214 Then bespake Lytell Johan
   To Much he gan say,
   'I dare lay my lyfe for to wedde,
   That monkes have brought our pay.

Then bespake Little John
To Much he did say,
'I dare lay my life as a pledge,
Those monks have
brought our pay.

215 'Make glad chere,' sayd Lytell Johan   *'Make glad cheer,' said Little John*
    'And frese our bowes of ewe,   *And draw our bows of yew,*
    And loke your hertes be seker and sad,   *And look your hearts be bold and strong,*

    Your strynges trusty and trewe.   *Your strings trusty and true.*

216 'The monke hath two and fifty,   *The monk hath two and fifty,*
    And seven somers full stronge;   *And seven sumpters full strong;*
    There rydeth no bysshop in this londe   *There rideth no bishop in this land*

    So ryally, I understond.   *So royally, I understand.*

217 'Brethern,' sayd Lytell Johan,   *'Brethern,' said Little John,*
    'Here are no more but we thre;   *'Here are no more but we three;*
    But we brynge them to dyner,   *Unless we bring them to dyner,*
    Our mayster dare we not se.   *Our master dare we not see.*

218 'Bende your bowes,' sayd Lytell Johan   *'Bend your bows,' said Little John*

    'Make all yon prese to stonde;   *Make all yon press to stand;*
    The formost monke, his lyfe and his deth,   *The foremost monk, his life and his death,*

    Is closed in my honde.   *Is closed in my hand.*

219 'Abyde, chorle monke,' sayd Lytell Johan   *'Abide, churl monk,' said Little John,*

    'No ferther that thou gone;   *'No farther may you run;*
    Yf thou doost, by dere worthy God,   *If thou dost, by dear worthy God,*
    Thy deth is in my honde.   *Thy death is in my hand.*

220 'And evyll thryfte on thy hede' sayd Lytell Johan   *'And evil fate on*
                                                                             thy head,' said Little John
    'Ryght under thy hattes bonde;   *Right under thy hat's band;*
    For thou hast made our mayster wroth,   *For thou hast made*
                                                                          our master wroth,
    He is fastynge so longe.'   *He is fasting so long.'*

221 'Who is your mayster?' sayd the monke;   *'Who is your master?'*
                                                                              said the monk;
    Lytell Johan sayd, 'Robyn Hode.'   *Little John said, 'Robin Hood.'*
    'He is a stronge thefe;' sayd the monke,   *'He is a strong thief,'*
                                                                             said the monk,
    'Of hym herd I never good.'   *Of him heard I never good.'*

222 'Thou lyest,' than sayd Lytell Johan   *'Thou liest,' then said Little John*
    'And that shall rewe the;   *'And that shall rue thee;*
    He is a yeman of the forest   *He is a yeoman of the forest*
    To dyne he hath bode the.'   *To dine he hath bid thee.'*

223 Much was redy with a bolte,   *Much was ready with a bolt,*
    Redly and anone,   *[Prepared to spare none].*
    He set the monke to-fore the brest,   *[He aimed for the monkés breast],*
    To the grounde that he can gone.   *To the ground lest he would gone.*

224 Of two and fifty wyght yonge yeman

    There abode not one,
    Saf a lytell page and a grome,
    To lede the somers with Lytel Johan.

Of two and fifty strong young yeoman
    There abode not one,
    Save a little page and a groom,
    To lead the sumpters with Little John.

225 They brought the monke to the lodge-dore,

    Whether he were loth or lefe,
    For to speke with Robyn Hode,
    Maugre in theyr tethe.

They brought the monk to the lodge-door,
    Whether he were loth or gave leave,
    For to speak with Robin Hood,
    In bitterness they set their teeth.

226 Robyn dyde adowne his hode,
    The monke whan that he se;
    The monke was not so curteyse,
    His hode then let he be.

Robin he cast off his hood,
    The monk when that he see;
    The monk was not so courteous;
    His hood then let he be.

227 'He is a chorle, mayster, by dere worthy God,'
    Than sayd Lytell Johan:
    'Thereof no force,' sayd Robyn,
    'For curteysy can he none.

'He is a churl, master, by dear worthy God,'
    Then said Little Johan:
    'Thereof no force,' said Robin,
    For courtesy can he none.

228 'How many men,' **than** sayd Robyn,
    'Had **nowe** this monke, Johan?'
    'Fyfty and two whan that we met,
    But many of them be gone.'

'How many men,' then said Robin,
    'Had now this monk, John?'
    Fifty and two when that we met,
    But many of them be gone.'

229 'Let blowe a horne,' sayd Robyn,   *'Let blow a horn,' said Robin,*
    'That felaushyp may us knowe;'   *That fellowship we may know;'*
    Seven score of wyght yeman   *Seven score of strong yeoman*
    Came prykynge on a rowe.   *Came out and stood in a row.*

230 And everych of them a good mantell   *And every one wore a good mantle*
    Of scarlet and of raye;   *Of scarlet and of array;*
    All they came to good Robyn,   *All they came to good Robin,*
    To wyte what he wolde say.   *To learn what he would say.*

231 They made the monke to wasshe and wype,   *They made the monk to wash and wipe,*
    And syt at his denere,   *And sit at his dinner,*
    Robyn Hode and Lytell Johan   *Robin Hood and Little John*
    They served him both in-fere.   *They served him as a pair.*

232 'Do gladly, monke,' sayd Robyn,   *'Do gladly, monk,' said Robin,*
    'Gramercy, syr,' sayd he.   *'Gramercy, sir,' said he.*
    'Where is your abbay, whan ye are at home,   *'Where is your abbey, when ye are at home,*
    And who is your avowe?'   *And to whom is your avowal?'*

233 'Saynt Mary Abbay,' sayde the monke,   *'Saint Mary's Abbey,' said the monk,*
    'Though I be symple here.'   *'Though I be simple here.'*
    'In what offyce,' sayd Robin.   *'In what office?' said Robin.*
    'Syr, the hye selerer.'   *'Sir, the high cellarer.'*

234 'Ye be the more welcome,' sayd Robyn,   'Ye be the more welcome,' said Robin,

   'So ever mote I the;   'So ever I greet such as thee;
   Fyll of the best wyne,' sayd Robyn,   Fill of the best wine,' said Robin,
   'This monke shall drynke to me.   'This monk shall drink to me.

235 'But I have grete mervayle,' sayd Robyn,   'But I greatly marvel,' said Robin,

   'Of all this longe day;   'Of all this longe day;
   I drede Our Lady be wroth with me,   I fear Our Lady be wroth with me,
   She sent me not my pay.'   She sent me not my pay.'

236 'Have no doute, mayster,' sayd Lytell Johan,   'Have no doubt, master,' said Little John,

   'Ye have no nede, I saye;   'Ye have no need, I say;
   This monke it hath brought, I dare well swere,   This monk it hath brought, I dare well swear,
   For he is of her abbay.'   For he is of her abbey.'

237 'And she was a borowe,' sayd Robyn,   'And she was a guarantor,' said Robin,

   'Between a knyght and me,   Between a knight and me,
   Of a lytell money that I hym lent,   Of a little money that I him lent,
   Under the grene-wode tree.   Under the greenwood tree.

238 'And yf thou hast that sylver ibrought,   'And if thou hast that silver brought,

    I pray the let me se;   I pray thee let me see;
    And I shall helpe the eftsones,   And I shall help the thereafter,
    Yf thou have nede to me.   If thou have need to me.'

239 The monke swore a full grete othe,   The monk swore a full great oath,
    With a sory chere,   With a sorry cheer,
    'Of the borowehode thou spekest to me   'Of the borrowing thou speakest to me
    Herde I never ere.'   I never heard before.'

240 'I make myn avowe to God,' sayde Robyn,   'I make mine avowe to God,' said Robin,
    'Monke, thou art to blame;   Monk, thou art to blame;
    For God is holde a rightwys man,   For God is held to be a righteous man,
    And so is his dame.   And so is his dame.

241 'Thou toldest with thyn owne tonge,   'Thou toldest with thine own tongue,
    Thou may not say nay,   Thou may not say nay,
    How thou arte her servaunt,   How thou arte her servant,
    And servest her every day.   And servest her every day.

242 'And thou art made her messengere,   'And thou art made her messenger,
    My money for to pay;   My money for to pay;
    Therfore I cun the more thanke   Therefore I can thee more thank
    Thou arte came at thy day.   Thou arte came at thy day.

243 'What is in your cofers?' sayd Robyn,   'What is in your coffers?' said Robin,

'Trewe than tell thou me:'   Truth then tell thou me.'
'Syr,' he sayd, 'twenty marke,   'Sir,' he said, 'twenty marks,
Al so mote I the.'   Also may I prosper thee.'

244 'Yf there be no more,' sayd Robyn,   'If there be no more,' said Robin,
'I wyll not one peny;   I will not take one penny;
Yf thou hast myster of ony more,   If thou hast need of any more,
Syr, more I shall lende to the.   Sir, more I shall lend to thee.

245 'And yf I fynde more,' sayd Robyn,   'And if I finde more,' said Robin,
'I-wys thou shalte it for gone;   I warn thou shalt it forgo;
For of thy spendynge-sylver, monke,   But of thy spending-silver, monk,
Thereof wyll I ryght none.   Thereof will I take none.

246 'Go nowe forthe, Lytell Johan,   'Go now forth, Little John,
And the trouth tell thou me;   And the truth tell thou me;
If there be no more but twenty marke,   If there be no more but twenty marks,

No peny that I se.'   No penny will I see.'

247 Lytell Johan spred his mantell downe,   Little John spread his mantle down,

As he had done before,   As he had done before,
And he tolde out of the monkes male   And counted from out of the monk's pack

Eyght hondred pounde and more.   Eight hundred pounds and more.

The Gest of Robyn Hode

248 Lytell Johan let it lye full styll,   *Little John let it lie full still,*
    And went to his mayster in hast;   *And went to his master in haste;*
    'Syr,' he sayd, 'the **monke*** is trewe ynowe,   *'Sir,' he said, 'the monk is true enough,*
    Our Lady hath doubled your cast.'   *Our Lady hath doubled your cast.'*

249 'I make myn avowe to God,' sayde Robyn.   *'I make mine avowe to God,' said Robin.*
    'Monke, that tolde I the: *'Monk, that told I thee:*
    Our Lady is the trewest woman   *Our Lady is the truest woman*
    That ever yet founde I me.   *That ever yet found I me.*

250 'By dere worthy God,' sayd Robyn,   *'By dear worthy God,' said Robin,*
    'To seche all Englond thorowe,   *To search all England through,*
    Yet founde I never to my pay   *Yet found I never to my pay*
    A moche better borowe.   *A much better guarantor.*

251 'Fyll of the best wyne, and do hym drynke,' sayd Robyn,   *'Fill of the best wine, and do it drink,' said Robin,*
    'And grete well thy lady hende,   *'And greet well thy lady kind,*
    And yf she have nede to Robyn Hode,   *And if she have need to Robin Hood,*
    A frende she shall hym fynde.   *A friend she shall him find.*

252 'And yf she nedeth ony more sylver,   *'And if she needs any more silver,*
    Come thou agayne to me,   *Come thou again to me,*
    And, by this token she hath me sent,   *And, by this token she hath me sent,*
    She shall have such thre.'   *She shall have it times three.'*

253 The monke was goynge to London ward,   *The monk was going to London-ward,*
    There to holde grete mote,   *There to hold a great meet,*
    The knyght that rode so hye on hors,   *The knight that rode so high on horse,*
    To brynge hym under fote.   *To bring him under their feet.*

254 'Whether be ye away?' sayd Robyn: *'Whither be ye away?' said Robin:*
    'Syr, to maners in this londe,   *'Sir, to manors in this land,*
    Too reken with our reves,   *To reckon with our thieves,*
    That have done moch wronge.'   *That have done much wrong.'*

255 'Come now forth, Lytell Johan,   *'Come now forth, Little John,*
    And harken to my tale;   *And harken to my tale;*
    A better yemen I knowe none,   *A better yeomen I know none,*
    To seke a monkes male.'   *To learn a monk's [toll].'*

256 'How moch is in yonder other corser?' sayd Robyn,   *'How much is on yonder other courser?' said Robin,*
    'The soth must we se:'   *'The truth must we see:'*
    'By Our Lady,' than sayd the monke,   *'By Our Lady,' then said the monk,*
    'That were no curteysye.   *That were no courtesy,*

257 'To bydde a man to dyner,   *'To bid a man to dinner,*
    And syth hym bete and bynde.'   *And then him beat and bind.'*
    'It is our olde maner,' sayd Robyn,   *'It is our old manner,' said Robin,*
    'To leve but lytell behynde.'   *'To leave but little behind.'*

The Gest of Robyn Hode

258 The monke toke the hors with spore, / The monk took the horse with spur,
No lenger wolde he abyde: / No longer would he abide:
'Aske to drynke,' than sayd Robyn, / 'Ask to drink,' then said Robin,
'Or that ye forther ryde.' / 'Before ye further ride.'

259 'Nay, for God,' than sayd the monke, / 'Nay, 'fore God,' then said the monk,
'Me reweth I cam so nere; / 'I rue I came so near;
For better chepe I myght have dyned / For better price I might have dined
In Blythe or in Dankestere.' / In Blythe or in Doncaster.'

260 'Grete well your abbot,' sayd Robyn, / 'Greet well your abbot,' said Robin,
'And your pryour, I you pray, / 'And your prior, I you pray,
And byd hym send me such a monke / And bid him send me such a monk
To dyner every day.' / To dinner every day.'

261 Now lete we that monke be styll, / Now let we that monk be still,
And speke we of that knyght: / And speak we of that knight:
Yet he came to holde his day, / How he came to hold his day,
Whyle that it was lyght. / While that it was light.

262 He dyde him streyt to Bernysdale, / He did him straight to Barnsdale,
Under the grene-wode tre, / Under the greenwood tree,
And he founde there Robyn Hode, / And there he found Robin Hood,
And all his mery meyne. / And his merry company.

263 The knyght lyght doune of his good palfray,   *The knight got down off his good palfrey,*

    Robyn whan he gan see,   *Robin when he did see,*
    So curteysly he dyde adoune his hode,   *So courteously he did off his hood,*

    And set hym on his knee.   *And set him on his knee.*

264 'God the save, Robyn Hode,   *'God thee save, Robin Hood,*
    And all this company:'   *And all this company.'*
    'Welcome be thou, gentyll knyght,   *'Welcome be thou, gentle knight,*
    And ryght welcome to me.'   *And right welcome to me.'*

265 Than bespake hym Robyn Hode,   *Than bespake him Robin Hood,*
    To that knyght so fre: *To that knight so free:*
    'What nede dryveth the to grene wode?   *'What need driveth thee to greenwood?*
    I praye the, syr knyght, tell me.   *I pray thee, Sir Knight, tell me.*

266 'And welcome be thou, gentyll knyght   *'And welcome be thou, gentle knight*
    Why hast thou be so longe?'   *Why has thou be so long?'*
    'For the abbot and the hye justyce   *'For the abbot and the high justice*
    Wolde have had my londe.'   *Would have had my land.'*

267 'Hast thou thy londe agayne?' sayd Robyn;   *'Hast thou thy land again?' said Robin;*

    'Treuth than tell thou me;'   *'Truth then tell thou me;'*
    'Ye, for God,' sayd the knyght,   *'Yes, 'fore God,' said the knight,*
    'And that thanke I God and the.   *'And that thank I God and thee.*

268 'But take not a grefe,' sayde the knyght,   'But take not a grief,' said the knight,
    That I have be so longe;   'That I have be so long;
    For as I came to grene wode   [For as I came to greenwood
    There I did tarry longe.   There I did tarry long.

268A **'For as I passed Wentesbridg***   'For as I passed Wentsbridge]
    I came by a wrastelynge   I came by a wrestling
    And there I holpe a pore yeman,   And there I helped a poor yeoman,
    With wronge was put behynde.'   With wrong was put behind.'

269 'Nay, for God,' sayd Robyn,   'Nay, 'fore God,' said Robin,
    'Syr knyght, that thanke I the;   'Sir knight, that thank I thee;
    What man that helpeth a good yeman,   What man that helpeth a good yeoman,
    His frende than wyll I be.'   His frende then will I be.'

270 'Have here foure hondred pounde,' than sayd the knyght,
        'Have here four hundred pound,' then said the knight,
    'The whiche ye lent to me;   'The which ye lent to me;
    And here is also twenty marke   And here is also twenty marks
    For your curteysy.'   For your courtesy.'

271 'Nay, for God,' than sayd Robyn,   'Nay, 'fore God,' then said Robin,
    'Thou broke it well for ay;   'Thou broke it well for aye;
    For Our Lady, by her **selerer**   For Our Lady, by her cellarer
    Hath sent to me my pay.   Hath sent to me my pay.

272 'And yf I toke it i-twyse,   'And if I took it twice,
    A shame it were to me;   A shame it were to me;
    But trewely, gentyll knyght,   But truly, gentle knight,
    Welcom arte thou to me.'   Welcome arte thou to me.'

273 Whan Robyn had tolde his tale,   When Robin had told his tale,
    He leugh and had good chere;   He laughed and had good cheer;
    'By my trouthe,' then sayd the knyght, 'By my troth,'
                                              then said the knight,
    'Your money is redy here.'   'Your money is already here.'

274 'Broke it well,' sayd Robyn,   'Use it well,' said Robin,
    'Thou gentyll knyght so fre,   'Thou gentle knight so free,
    And welcome be thou, gentyll knyght,   And welcome be thou,
                                                gentle knight,
    Under my trystell-tre.   Under my tristel-tree.

275 'But what shall these bowes do?' sayd Robyn, 'But what shall these
                                                bowes do?' said Robin,
    'And these arowes ifedred fre?'   And these arrows feathered free?'
    'By God,' than sayd the knyght,   'By God,' then said the knight,
    'A pore present to the.'   A poor present to thee.'

276 'Come now forth, Lytell Johan,   'Come now forth, Little John,
    And go to my treasure,   And go to my treasury,
    And brynge me there foure hondred pounde; And bring me there
                                                four hundred pounds;
    The monke over-tolde it me.   The monk over-tolde it me.

277 'Have here foure hondred pounde,   'Have here four hundred pound,
    Thou gentyll knyght and trewe,   Thou gentle knight and true,
    And bye hors and harnes good,   And buy horse and harness good,
    And gylte thy spores all newe.   And gild thy spurs all new.

278 'And yf thou fayle ony spendynge,   'And if thou fail any spending-money,
    Com to Robyn Hode,   Come to Robin Hood,
    And by my trouth thou shalt none fayle,   And by my troth thou shalt none fail,
    The whyles I have any good.   The while I have any good.

279 'And broke well thy foure hondred pound,   'And use well thy four hundred pound,
    Whiche I lent to the,   Which I lent to thee,
    And make thy selfe no more so bare,   And make thyself no more so bare,
    By the counsell of me.'   By the counsel of me.'

280 Thus than holpe hym good Robyn,   Thus than helped him good Robin,
    The knyght all of this care: The knight all of this care:
    God, that syt in heven hye,   God, that sit in heaven high,
    Graunte us well to fare!   Grant us well to fare!

The Fyfth Fytte   The Fifth Fit

281 Now hath the knyght his leve i-take,   Now hath the knight his leave taken,
    And wente hym on his way;   And went him on his way;
    Robyn Hode and his mery men   Robin Hood and his merry men
    Dwelled styll full many a day.   Dwelled still full many a day.

282 Lyth and lysten, gentil men,   Stop and listen, gentlemen,
    And herken what I say,   And hearken what I say,
    How the proude sheryfe of Notyngham   How the proud Sheriff of Nottingham
    Dyde crye a full fayre play;   Did cry a full fair game;

283 That all the best archers of the north   That all the best archers of the north
    Sholde come upon a day,   Should come upon a day,
    And **he** that shoteth all ther best   And he that shot all there best
    The game shall bere a way.   The game should bear away.

284 'He that shoteth **all theyre** best,   'He that shot all there best,
    Furthest fayre and lowe,   Furthest fair and wide,
    At a payre of fynly buttes,   At a pair of butts,
    Under the grene-wode shawe,   Under the greenwood side,

285 'A ryght good arowe he shall have,   'A right good arrow he shall have,
    The shaft of sylver whyte,   The shaft of silver white,
    The hede and the feders of ryche rede golde,   The head and the feathers of riche red gold,
    In Englond is none lyke.'   In England is none like.'

286 This than herde good Robyn,   This then heard good Robin,
    Under his trystell-tre;   Under his tristel-tree;
    'Make you redy, ye wyght yonge men;   'Make you ready, ye strong young men;
    That shotynge wyll I se.   That shooting will I see.

The Gest of Robyn Hode

287 'Buske you, my mery yonge men,   'Get ready, my merry young men,
     Ye shall go with me;   Ye shall go with me;
     And I wyll wete the shryves fayth,   And I will know the sheriff's faith,
     Trewe and yf he be.'   True and if he be.'

288 Whan they had theyr bowes i-bent,   When they had their bows bent,
     Theyr takles fedred fre,   Their tackles feathered free,
     Seven score of wyght yonge men   Seven score of strong young men
     Stode by Robyns kne.   Stood by Robin's knee.

289 Whan they cam to Notyngham,   When they came to Nottingham,
     The buttes were fayre and longe;   The butts were fair and long;
     Many was the bolde archere   Many was the bold archer
     That shoted with bowes stronge.   That shot with bowés strong.

290 'There shall but syx shote with me;   'There shall but six shot with me;
     The other shal kepe my **hede**   The others shall guard my head
     And stande with good bowes bent,   And stand with good bowes bent,
     That I be not desceyved.'   That I be not deceived.'

291 The fourth outlawe his bowe gan bende,   The fourth outlaw his bow did bend,
     And that was Robyn Hode,   And that was Robin Hood,
     And that behelde the proud sheryfe,   And that beheld the proud sheriff,
     All by the but **as** he stode.   All by the butt as he stood.

292 Thryes Robyn shot about,   Thrice Robin shot about,
     And alway they **slist** the wand,   And always they sliced the wand,
     And so dyde good Gylberte   And so did good Gilbert
     Wyth the whyte hande.   With the white hand.

293 Lytell Johan and good Scathelock
　　Were archers good and fre;
　　Lytell Much and good Reynolde,
　　The worste wolde they not be.

294 Whan they had shot aboute,
　　These archours fayre and good,
　　Evermore was the best,
　　For soth, Robyn Hode.

295 Hym was delyvered the good arowe,

　　For best worthy was he;
　　He toke the yeft so curteysly,
　　To grene wode wolde he.

296 They cryed out on Robyn Hode,
　　And grete hornes gan they blowe,
　　'Wo worth the, treason!' sayd Robyn,
　　'Full evyl thou art to knowe.

297 'And wo be thou! thou proude sheryf,

　　Thus gladdynge thy gest;
　　Other wyse thou behote me
　　In yonder wylde forest.

Little John and good Scathelock
Were archers good and free;
Little Much and good Reynold,
The worst would they not be.

When they had shot about,
These archers fair and good,
Evermore was the best,
Forsooth, Robin Hood.

To him was delivered
the good arrow,
For best worthy was he;
He toke the gift so courteously,
To greenwood would he.

They cried out on Robin Hood,
And great horns began to blow,
'Woe to thee, treason!' said Robin,
'Full evil thou art to know.

'And woe be thou!
thou proud sheriff,
Thus greeting thy guest;
Otherwise thou promised me
In yonder wild forest.

298 'But had I the in grene wode,   *But had I thee in greenwood,*
      Under my trystell-tre,   *Under my tristel-tree,*
      Thou sholdest leve me a better wedde   *Thou shouldest leave me a better guarantee*
      Than thy trewe lewte.'   *Than thy true loyalty.'*

299 Full many a bowe there was bent   *Full many a bow there was bent*
      And arowes let they glyde;   *And arrows let they glide;*
      Many a kyrtell there was rent,   *Many a kirtle there was rent,*
      And hurt many a syde.   *And hurt many a side.*

300 The outlawes shot was so stronge   *The outlaws' shot was so stronge*
      That no man myght them dryve,   *That no man might [make them flee],*
      And the proud sheryfes men,   *And the proud Sheriff's men,*
      They fled away full blyve.   *They fled away with speed.*

301 Robyn sawe the busshement to-broke,   *Robin saw the ambush coming,*
      In grene wode he wolde have be;   *In greenwood he sooner would be;*
      Many an arowe there was shot,   *Many an arrow there was shot,*
      Amonge that company.   *Among that company.*

302 Lytell Johan was hurte full sore,   *Little John was hurt full sore,*
      With an arowe in his kne,   *With an arrow in his knee,*
      That he myght neyther go nor ryde;   *That he might neither walk nor ride;*
      It was full grete pyte.   *It was a great pity.*

303 'Mayster,' then sayd Lytell Johan,   *'Master,' then said Little John,*
      'If ever thou lovest me,   *'If ever thou lovest me,*
      And for that ylke Lordes love   *And for that very Lordés love*
      That dyed upon a tre,   *That died upon a tree,*

304 'And for the medes of my servyce,   'And for the reward of my service,
    That I have served the,   That I have served thee,
    Lete never the proude sheryf   Let never the proud Sheriff
    Alyve now fynde me.   Alive now find me.

305 'But take out thy browne swerde,   'But take out thy brown sword,
    And smyte all of my hede,   And smite all off my head,
    And gyve me woundes depe and wyde;   And give me wounds deep and wide;
    No lyfe on me be lefte.'   No life on me be left.'

306 'I wolde not that,' sayd Robyn,   'I would not that,' said Robin,
    'Johan, that thou were slawe,   'John, that thou were slew,
    For all the golde in mery Englonde,   For all the gold in merry England,
    Though it lay now on a rawe.'   Though it lay now on a row.'

307 'God forebede,' sayd Lytell Much,   'God forbid,' said Little Much,
    'That dyed on a tre,   'That died on a tree,
    That thou sholdest, Lytell Johan,   That thou shouldest, Little John,
    Parte our company.'   Part our company.'

308 Up he toke hym on his backe,   Up he took him on his back,
    And bare hym well a myle;   And bare him well a mile;
    Many a tyme he layd hym downe,   Many a time he laid him down,
    And shot another whyle.   And shot another while.

309 Then was there a fayre castell,   Then was there a fair castle,
    A lytell within the wode;   A little within the wood;
    Double-dyched it was about,   Double-ditched it was about,
    And walled, by the rode.   And walléd, by the rood.

310 And there dwelled that gentyll knyght,

    Syr Rychard at the Lee,
    That Robyn had lent his good,
    Under the grene-wode tree.

311 In he toke good Robyn,
    And all his company;
    'Welcome be thou, Robyn Hode,
    Welcome arte thou to me.

312 'And moche thanke the of thy confort,

    And of thy courteysye,
    And of thy grete kyndenesse,
    Under the grene-wode tre.

313 'I love no man in all this worlde
    So much as I do the;
    For all the proud sheryf of Notyngham,

    Ryght here shalt thou be.

314 'Shyt the gates, and draw the brydge,

    And let no man come in,
    And arme you well, and make you redy,

    And to the **walle** ye wynne.

And there dwelled
hat gentle knight,
Sir Richard at the Lee,
That Robin had lent his good,
Under the greenwood tree.

In he took good Robin,
And all his company;
'Welcome be thou, Robin Hood,
Welcome art thou to me;

'And much thank thee
of thy comfort,
And of thy courtesy,
And of thy great kindness,
Under the greenwood tree.

'I love no man in all this world
So much as I do thee;
For all the proud
Sheriff of Nottingham,
Safe here shalt thou be.

'Shut the gates, and
draw the bridge,
And let no man come in,
And arm you well,
and make you ready,
And to the wall be gone.

315 'For one thynge, Robyn, I the behote;	*For one thing, Robin, I thee promised;*
I swere by Saynt Quyntyne,	*I swear by Saint Quentin,*
These **twelve*** dayes thou wonnest with me,	*These twelve days thou shall stay with me,*
To soupe, ete, and dyne.'	*To soup, eat, and dine.'*
316 Bordes were layde, and clothes were spredde,	*Boards were laid, and clothes were spread,*
Redely and anone;	*Speedily and soon;*
Robyn Hode and his mery men	*Robin Hood and his merry men*
To mete can they gone.	*To dinner then have gone.*

The VI Fytte

The Sixth Fit

317 Lythe and lysten, gentylmen,	*Stop and listen, gentlemen,*
And herkyn to your songe;	*And hearken to your song;*
Howe the proude shyref of Notyngham,	*How the proud Sheriff of Nottingham,*
And men of armys stronge	*And men of armés strong*
318 Full fast cam to the hye shyref,	*Full fast came to the high sheriff,*
The countre up to route,	*The country up to rout,*
And they besette the knyghtes castell,	*And they beset the knight's castle,*
The walles all aboute.	*The wallés all about.*

The Gest of Robyn Hode

319 The proude shyref loude gan crye,
 And sayde, 'Thou traytour knight,
 Thou kepest here the kynges **enemye**,

 Agaynst the **lawes** and ryght.'

320 'Syr, I wyll avowe that I have done,
 The dedys **thou** here be dyght,
 Upon all the landes that I have,
 As I am a trewe knyght.'

321 'Wende furth, sirs, on your way,
 And do no more to me
 Tyll ye wyt oure kynges wille,
 What he wyll say to the.'

322 The shyref thus had his answere,
 Without any lesynge;
 Furth he yede to London towne
 All for to tel our kinge.

323 There he telde him of that knight,
 And eke of Robyn Hode,
 And also of the bolde archars,
 That **were soo noble** and gode.

*The proud Sheriff loud did cry,
And said, 'Thou traitor knight,
Thou keepest here
the King's enemy,
Against the laws and right.'*

*'Sir, I will avow that I have done,
The deeds thou here recite,
Upon all the lands that I have,
As I am a true knight.*

*'Go forth, sirs, on your way,
And do no more to me
Till you know our king's will,
What he will say to thee.'*

*The Sheriff thus had his answer,
Without any hiding;
Forth he went to London town
All for to tell our king.*

*There he told him of that knight,
And also of Robin Hood,
And also of the bold archers,
That were so noble and good.*

324 'He wyll avowe that he hath done,   'He will avow that he hath done,
     To mayntene the outlawes stronge;   To maintain the outlaws strong;
     He **wolde** be lorde, and set you at nought,   He would be lord, and set you at nought,
     In all the northe londe.'   In all the north land.'

325 'I wil be at Notyngham,' saide our kynge,   'I will be at Nottingham,' said our king,
     'Within this fourteenyght,   Within this fortnight,
     And take I wyll Robyn Hode,   And take I will Robin Hood,
     And so I wyll that knight.   And so I will that knight.

326 '**Go home, thou proud sheryf**   'Go home, thou proud Sheriff
     'And do as I byd the;   And do as I bid thee;
     And ordeyn gode archers ynowe,   And organize good archers enough,
     Of all the wyde contre.'   Of all the wide country.'

327 The shyref had his leve i-take,   The Sheriff did his leave take,
     And went hym on his way,   And went him on his way,
     And Robyn Hode to grene wode,   And Robin Hood went to greenwood,
     Upon a certen day.   Upon a certain day.

328 And Lytel John was hole of the arowe   And Little John was healed of the arrow
     That shot was in his kne,   That shot was in his knee,
     And dyd hym streyght to Robyn Hode,   And did him straight to Robin Hood,
     Under the grene-wode tree.   Under the greenwood tree.

329 Robyn Hode walked in the forest,   *Robin Hood walked in the forest,*
　　Under the levys grene;   *Under the leaves green;*
　　The proude shyref of Notyngham   *The proud Sheriff of Nottingham*
　　Therfore he had grete tene.   *Therefore he had great grief.*

330 The shyref there fayled of Robyn Hode,   *The sheriff there failed of Robin Hood,*
　　He myght not have his pray;   *He might not have his prey;*
　　Than he awayted this gentyll knyght,   *Then he awaited this gentle knight,*
　　Bothe by nyght and day.   *Both by night and day.*

331 Ever he wayted this gentyll knyght,   *Ever he waited this gentle knight,*
　　Syr Richarde at the Lee,   *Sir Richard at the Lee,*
　　As he went on haukynge by the ryver-syde,   *As he went on hawking by the river side,*
　　And lete **his** haukes flee.   *And let his hawkés flee.*

332 Toke he there this gentyll knight,   *Took he there this gentle knight,*
　　With men of armys stronge,   *With men of armés strong,*
　　And led **hym home** to Notyngham warde,   *And led him home to Nottingham's ward,*
　　Bounde bothe fote and hande.   *Bound both foot and hand.*

333 The sheref sware a full grete othe   *The Sheriff swore a full great oath*
　　Bi hym that dyed on rode,   *By him that died on rood,*
　　He had lever than an hundred pound   *He had sooner than an hundred pound*
　　That he had Robyn Hode.   *That he had Robin Hood.*

334 This harde the knyghtes wyfe,
   A fayr lady and a free;
   She set hir on a gode palfrey,
   To grene wode anone rode she.

This heard the knightés wife,
A fair lady and a free;
She set her on a good palfrey,
To greenwood anon rode she.

335 Whanne she cam in the forest,
   Under the grene-wode tree,
   Fonde she there Robyn Hode,
   And al his fayre mene.

When she came in the forest,
Under the greenwood tree,
Found she there Robin Hood,
And all his fair company.

336 'God the save, gode Robyn,
   And all thy company;
   For Our dere lady **love**,
   A bone graunte thou me.

'God thee save, good Robin,
And all thy company;
For our dear Lady's love,
A boon grant thou me.

337 '**Late thou** never my wedded lorde
   Shamefully slayne be;
   He is fast **bounde** to Notingham warde,

   For the love of the.'

'Let thou never my wedded lord
Shamefully slain be;
He is fast bound
to Nottingham's ward,
For the love of thee.'

338 Anone then saide goode Robyn
   To that lady **fre**,
   What man hath your lorde i-take?
   ....*

Anon then said good Robin
To that lady free,
'What man hath your lord taken?
[And where may he now be?']

339 ....*
   'For soth as I the say;
   He is nat yet thre myles
   Passed on his way.

['The Sheriff hath my lord taken,]
For sooth as I thee say;
He is not yet three miles
Passed on his way.'

The Gest of Robyn Hode

340 Up than sterte gode Robyn,
   As man that had ben wode;
   'Buske you, my mery **yonge** men,

   For hym that dyed on rode.

341 'And he that this sorowe forsaketh,
   By hym that dyed on tre,
   Shall he never in grene wode
   No lenger dwel with me.'

342 Sone there were gode bowes bent,
   Mo than seven score;
   Hedge ne dyche spared they none
   That was them before.

343 'I make myn avowe to God,' sayde Robyn,

   'The **sherif*** wolde I fayne see;
   And if I may hym take,
   I-quyt then shall it be.'

344 And whan they came to Notingham,

   They walked in the strete;
   And with the proude sherif i-wys
   Sone can they mete.

Up then started good Robin,
As man that had been mad;
'Get ready now, my merry young men,
For him that died on rood.

'And he that this duty forsaketh,
By him that died on tree,
Shall he never in greenwood
No longer dwell with me.'

Soone there were good bows bent,
More than seven score;
Hedge nor ditch spared they none
That was them before.

'I make mine avowe to God,' said Robin,
The sheriff would I fain see;
And if I may him take,
Quit then shall it be.'

And when they came to Nottingham,
They walked in the street;
And with the proud Sheriff I know
Soon then they did meet.

The Gest of Robyn Hode

345 'Abyde, thou proude sherif,' he sayde,   'Abide, thou proud Sheriff,' he said,

    'Abyde, and speke with me;   'Abide, and speak with me;
    Of some tidinges of oure kinge   Of some tidings of our king
    I wolde fayne here of the.   I would fain hear of thee.

346 'This seven yere, by dere worthy God,   'This seven year, by dear worthy God,

    Ne yede I **so** fast on fote;   Never ran I so fast on foot;
    I make myn avowe to God, thou proude sherif,   I make mine avowe to God, thou proud Sheriff,
    It is nat for thy gode.'   It is not for thy good.'

347 Robyn bent a full goode bowe,   Robin bent a full good bow,

    An arrowe he drowe at wyll;   An arrow he drew at will;
    He hit so the proude sherife   He hit so the proud Sheriff
    Upon the grounde he lay full still.   Upon the ground he lay full still.

348 And or he myght up aryse,   And ere he might up arise,

    On his fete to stonde,   On his feet to stand,
    He smote of the sherifs hede   He smote off the Sheriff's head
    With his brighte bronde.   With his bright brand.

349 'Lye thou there, thou proude sherife,   'Lie thou there, thou proud Sheriff,

    Evyll mote thou **cheve**!   Evil might thou achieve!
    There myght no man to the truste   There might no man to thee trust
    The whyles thou were a lyve.'   The while thou were alive.'

350 His men drewe out theyr bryght swerdes,

    That were so sharpe and kene,
    And layde on the sheryves men,
    And dryved them down bydene.

351 Robyn stert to that knyght,
    And cut a two his **hoode**,*
    And toke hym in his hand a bowe,
    And bad hym by hym stonde.

352 'Leve thy hors the behynde,
    And lerne for to renne;
    Thou shalt with me to grene wode,
    Through myre, mosse, and fenne.

353 'Thou shalt with me to grene wode,
    Without ony leasynge,
    Tyll that I have gete the grace
    Of Edwarde, our comly kynge.'

The VII Fytte

354 The kynge came to Notynghame,
    With knyghtes in grete araye,
    For to take that gentyll knyght
    And Robyn Hode, and yf he may.

His men drew out their bright swords,
That were so sharp and keen,
And laid on the Sheriff's men,
And drove them [from the green].

Robin started to that knight,
And cut in two his hood,
And took him in his hand a bow,
And bade him by him stand.

'Leave thy horse thee behind,
And learn for to run;
Thou shalt with me to greenwood,
Through mire, moss, and fen.

'Thou shalt with me to greenwood,
Without any lying,
Till that I have gotten the grace
Of Edward, our comely king.'

The Seventh Fit

The King came to Nottingham,
With knights in great array,
For to take that gentle knight
And Robin Hood, if he may.

355 He asked men of that countre
   After Robyn Hode,
   And after that gentyll knyght,
   That was so bolde and stout.

356 Whan they had tolde hym the case
   Our kynge understonde ther tale,
   And seased in his honde
   The knyghtes londes all.

357 All the passe of Lancasshyre
   He went both ferre and nere,
   Tyll he came to Plomton Parke;
   He faylyed many of his dere.

358 There our kynge was wont to se
   Herdes many one,
   He coud unneth fynde one dere,
   That bare ony good horne.

359 The kynge was wonder wroth withall,

   And swore by the Trynyte,
   'I wolde I had Robyn Hode,
   With eyen I myght hym se.

*He asked men of that country
After Robin Hood,
And after that gentle knight,
That was so bold and stout.*

*When they had tolde him the case
Our king understood their tale,
And seized in his hand
The knight's landés all.*

*All the passes of Lancashire
He went both far and near,
Till he came to Plumpton Park;
He failed to find many deer.*

*There our King was wont to see
Herds many one,
He could not find even one deer,
That bare any good horn.*

*The King was wondrous
wroth withall,
And swore by the Trinity,
'I would I had Robin Hood,
With my eyes I might him see.*

360 'And he that wolde smyte of the knyghtes hede,

    And brynge it to me,
    He shall have the knyghtes londes,
    Syr Rycharde at the Le.

361 'I gyve it hym with my charter,
    And sele it **with** my honde,
    To have and holde for ever more,
    In all mery Englonde.'

362 Than bespake a fayre olde knyght,
    That was treue in his fay;
    'A, my leege lorde the kynge,
    One worde I shall you say.

363 'There is no man in this countre
    May have the knyghtes londes,
    Whyle Robyn Hode may ryde or gone,

    And bere a bowe in his hondes,

364 'That he ne shall lese his hede,
    That is the best ball in his hode:
    Give it no man, my lorde the kynge,
    That ye wyll any good.'

'And he that would smite off the knight's head,

    And bring it unto me,
    He shall have the knight's lands,
    Sir Richard at the Lee.

'I give it him with my charter,
    And seal it with my hand,
    To have and hold forevermore,
    In all merry England.'

Then bespake a fair old knight,
    That was true in his faith;
    'Ah, my liege lord the King,
    One word I shall you say.

'There is no man in this country
    May have the knight's lands
    While Robin Hood may ride or go,
    And bear a bow in his hands,

'That he shall not lose his head,
    That is the best ball in his hood:
    Give it no man, my lord the King,
    That ye wish any good.'

365 Halfe a yere dwelled our comly kynge
    In Notyngham, and well more;
    Coude he not here of Robyn Hode,
    In what countre that he were.

366 But alway went good Robyn
    By halke and eke by hyll,
    And always slewe the kynges dere,
    And welt them at his wyll.

367 Than bespake a proude fostere,
    That stode by our kynges kne:
    'Yf ye wyll se good Robyn,
    Ye must do after me.

368 'Take fyve of the best knyghtes
    That be in your lede,
    And **walke** downe by your abbay,
    And gete you monkes wede.

369 'And I wyll be your ledes-man,
    And lede you the way,
    And or ye come to Notyngham,
    Myn hede then dare I lay,

Half a year dwelled our comely King
    In Nottingham, and well more;
    Could he not hear of Robin Hood,
    In what country that he were.

But always went good Robin
    By nitch and also by hill,
    And always slew the King's deer,
    And took them at his will.

Then bespoke a proud forester,
    That stood by our King's knee:
    'If ye will see good Robin,
    Ye must do after me.

'Take five of the best knights
    That be in your forces,
    And walk down by your abbey,
    And get you monk´s clothes.

'And I will be your leadsman,
    And lead you on the way,
    And ere ye come to Nottingham,
    Mine head then dare I lay,

The Gest of Robyn Hode

370 'That ye shall mete with good Robyn,   'That ye shall meet with good Robin,
    On lyve yf that he be;   Alive if that he be;
    Or ye come to Notyngham,   Ere ye come to Nottingham,
    With eyen ye shall hym se.'   With eyes ye shall him see.'

371 Full hastly our kynge was dyght,   Full hastily our King prepared,
    So were his knyghtes fyve,   So did his knights five,
    Everych of them in monkes wede,   Every one of them in monk's clothes,
    And hasted them **thyder** blyth.   And hasted them there blythe.

372 Our kynge was grete above his cole,   Our King was great above his cowl,
    A brode hat on his crowne,   A broad hat on his crown,
    Ryght as he were abbot-lyke,   Right as he were abbot-like,
    They rode up in-to the towne.   They rode up into the town.

373 Styf botes our kynge had on,   Stiff boots our King had on,
    Forsoth as I you say;   Forsooth as I you say;
    He rode syngynge to grene wode,   He rode singing to greenwood,
    The covent was clothed in graye.   The company was clothed in gray.

374 His male-hors and his grete somers   His pack-horse and his great sumpters
    Folowed our kynge behynde,   Followed our King behind,
    Tyll they came to grene wode,   Till they came to greenwood
    A myle under the lynde.   A mile under the lind.

375 There they met with good Robyn,
   Stondynge on the waye,
   And so dyde many a bolde archere,
   For soth as I you say.

376 Robyn toke the kynges hors,
   Hastely in that stede,
   And sayd, 'Syr abbot, by your leve,
   A whyle ye must abyde.

377 'We be yemen of this foreste,
   Under the grene-wode tre;
   We lyve by our kynges dere,
   ....*

378 'And ye have chyrches and rentes both,

   And gold full grete plente;
   Gyve us some of your spendynge
   For saynt charyte.'

379 Than bespake our cumly kynge,
   Anone than sayd he;
   'I brought no more to grene wode
   But forty pounde with me.

380 'I have layne at Notyngham
   This fourtynyght with our kynge,
   And spent I have full moche good,
   On many a grete lordynge.

There they met with good Robin,
Standing on the way,
And so bold many a bold archer,
Forsooth as I you say.

Robin took the King's horse,
Hastily in that stead,
And said, 'Sir abbot, by your leave,
A while ye must abide.

'We be yeomen of this forest,
Under the greenwood tree;
We live by our King's deer,
[No other land have we.]

'And ye have churches
and rents both,
And gold full great plenty;
Give us some of your spending
For holy charity.'

Than bespoke our comely King,
Anon then said he;
'I brought no more to greenwood
But forty pounds with me.

I have lain at Nottingham
This fortnight with our King,
And spent I have full much good,
On many a great lordling.

The Gest of Robyn Hode

381 'And I have but forty pounde,
    No more than have I me;
    But yf I had an hondred pounde,
    I **vouch it halfe*** on the.'

'And I have but forty pounds,
    No more then have I me;
    But if I had an hundred pounds,
    I vouch it half on thee.'

382 Robyn toke the forty pounde,
    And departed it in two partye;
    Halfandell he gave his mery men,
    And bad them mery to be.

Robin took the forty pound,
    And parted in in half;
    Half he gave his merry men,
    And bade them merry to be.

383 Full curteysly Robyn gan say;
    'Syr, have this for your spendyng;
    We shall mete another day.'
    'Gramercy,' than sayd our kynge.

Full courteously Robin did say;
    'Sir, have this for your spending;
    We shall meet another day.'
    'Gramercy,' then said our King.

384 'But well the greteth Edwarde, our kynge,

    And sent to the his seale,
    And byddeth the com to Notyngham,

    Both to mete and mele.'

'But well thee greeteth Edward, our King,
    And sent to thee his seal,
    And bids thee come to Nottingham,
    Both to meat and meal.'

385 He toke out the brode **targe***,
    And **sone*** he lete hym se;
    Robyn coud his courteysy,
    And set hym on his kne.

He took out the broad [shield],
    And soon he let him see;
    Robin knew his courtesy,
    And set him on his knee.

386 'I love no man in all the worlde
    So well as I do my kynge;
    Welcome is my lordes seale;
    And monke, for thy tydenge,

387 'Syr abbot, for thy tydynges,
    To day thou shalt dyne with me,
    For the love of my kynge,
    Under my trystell-tre.'

388 Forth he lad our comly kynge,
    Full fayre by the honde;
    Many a dere there was slayne,
    And full fast dyghtande.

389 Robyn toke a full grete horne,
    And loude he gan blowe;
    Seven score of wyght yonge men
    Came redy on a rowe.

390 All they kneled on theyr kne,
    Full fayre before Robyn;
    The kynge sayd hym selfe untyll,
    And swore by Saynt Austyn,

391 'Here is a wonder semely syght;
    Me thynketh, by Goddes pyne,
    His men are more at his byddynge
    Then my men be at myn.'

'I love no man in all the world
    So well as I do my King;
    Welcome is my lord's seal;
    And monk, for thy tidings,

'Sir abbot, for thy tidings,
    Today thou shalt dine with me,
    For the love of my King,
    Under my tristel-tree.'

Forth he led our comely King,
    Full fair by the hand;
    Many a deer there was slain,
    And full fast put in pan.

Robin took a full great horn,
    And loud he did blow;
    Seven score of strong young men
    Came ready on a row.

They all kneeled on their knee,
    Full fair before Robin;
    The King said himself until,
    And swore by Saint Austin,

'Here is a wondrous seemly sight;
    Me thinketh, by God's pain,
    His men are more at his bidding
    Then my men be at mine.'

392 Full hastly was theyr dyner idyght *Full quickly was their dinner made*
    And therto gan they gone; *And thereto were they gone;*
    They served our kynge with al theyr myght, *They served our King with all their might,*
    Both Robyn and Lytell Johan. *Both Robin and Little John.*

393 Anone before our kynge was set *Anon before our King was set*
    The fatte venyson, *The fat venison,*
    The good whyte brede, the good rede wyne, *The good white bread, the good red wine,*
    And therto the fyne ale and browne. *And then the fine ale and brown.*

394 'Make good chere,' said Robyn, *'Make good cheer,' said Robin,*
    'Abbot, for charyte; *'Abbot, for charity;*
    And for this ylke tydynge, *And for this very tiding,*
    Blyssed mote thou be. *Blessed might thou be.*

395 'Now shalte thou se what lyfe we lede, *'Now shalt thou see what life we lead,*
    Or thou hens wende; *Ere thou hence journey;*
    Than thou may enfourme our kynge, *Then thou may inform our King,*
    Whan ye togyder lende.' *When ye together be.'*

396 Up they sterte all in hast, *Up they started all in haste,*
    Theyr bowes were smartly bent; *Their bows were smartly nocked;*
    Our kynge was never so sore agast *Our King was never so sore aghast*
    He wende to have be shente. *He feared to have been shot.*

397 Two yerdes there were up set,
    Thereto gan they gange;
    By fyfty pase, our kynge sayd,
    The merkes were to longe.

398 On every syde a rose-garlonde,
    They shot under the lyne;
    'Who so faileth of the rose-garlonde,' sayd Robyn,
    'His takyll he shall tyne.

399 'And yelde it to his mayster,
    Be it never so fyne;
    For no man wyll I spare,
    So drynke I ale or wyne:

400 'And bere a buffet on his hede,
    I-wys ryght all bare:'
    And all that fell in Robyns lote,
    He smote them wonder sare.

401 Twyse Robyn shot aboute,
    And ever he cleved the wande,
    And so dyde good Gylberte
    With the **good whyte** hande.

402 Lytell Johan and good Scathelocke,
    For nothynge wolde they spare;
    When they fayled of the garlonde,
    Robyn smote them full sore.

Two yards there were up set,
    Thereto they did gang;
    By fifty paces, our King said,
    The marks were set too long.

On every side a rose-garland,
    They shot under the trees;
    'Who so faileth of the rose-garland,' said Robin,
    'His tackle he shall lose.

'And yield it to his master,
    Be it never so fine;
    For no man will I spare,
    So drink I ale or wine:

'And bear a buffet on his head,
    I order that all bear' —
    And all that fell in Robin's lot,
    He smote them wondrous sore.

Twice Robin shot aboute,
    And ever he cleft the wand,
    And so did good Gilbert
    With the good white hand.

Little John and good Scathelock,
    For nothing would they spare;
    When they failed of the garland,
    Robin smote them full sore.

403 At the last shot that Robyn shot,
    For all his frendes fare,
    Yet he fayled of the garlonde
    Thre fyngers and mare.

404 Then bespake good Gylberte,
    And thus he gan say;
    'Mayster,' he sayd, 'your takyll is lost,
    Stande forth and take your pay.'

405 'If it be so,' sayd Robyn,
    'That may no better be,
    Syr abbot, I delyver the myn arowe,
    I pray the, syr, serve thou me.'

406 'It falleth not for myn ordre,' sayd our kynge,
    'Robyn, by thy leve,
    For to smyte no good yeman,
    For doute I sholde hym greve.'

407 'Smyte on boldely,' sayd Robyn,
    'I give the large leve':
    Anone our kynge, with that worde,
    He folde up his sleve,

At the last shot that Robin shot,
    For all his band's cheers,
    Yet he failed of the garland
    Three fingers and more.

Then bespake good Gilbert,
    And thus he did say;
    'Master,' he said, 'your tackle is lost,
    'Stand forth and take your pay.'

'If it be so,' said Robin,
    That may no better be,
    Sir abbot, I deliver thee mine arrow,
    I pray thee, sir, serve thou me.'

'It falleth not for mine order,' said our King,
    'Robin, by thy leave,
    For to smite no good yeoman,
    For fear I should him grieve.'

'Smite on boldly,' said Robin,
    I give thee large leve.'
    Anon our King, with that word,
    He folded up his sleeve,

408 And sych a buffet he gave Robyn,   And such a buffet he gave Robin,
   To grounde he yede full nere: To ground he fell full near:
   'I make myn avowe to God,' sayd Robyn,   'I make mine avowe to God,' said Robin,

   'Thou arte a stalworthe frere.   'Thou art a stalwart friar.

409 'There is pith in thyn arme,' sayd Robyn,   'There is pith in thine arm,' said Robin,

   'I trowe thou canst well shote:'   'I ken thou canst well shoot:'
   Thus our kynge and Robyn Hode   Thus our King and Robin Hood
   Togeder than they met.   Together then they met.

410 Robyn behelde our comly kynge   Robin beheld our comely King
   Wystly in the face,   Squarely in the face,
   So dyde Syr Rycharde at the Le,   So did Sir Richard at the Lee,
   And kneled down in that place.   And kneeled down in that place.

411 And so dyde all the wylde outlawes,   And so did all the wild outlaws,
   Whan they se them knele;   When they saw them kneel;
   'My lorde the kynge of Englonde,   'My lorde the King of England,
   Now I knowe you well.'   Now I know you well.'

412 **'Mercy then, Robyn', sayd our kynge,***   'Mercy then, Robin,' said our King,

   'Under your trystyll-tre,   'Under your tristel-tree,
   Of thy goodnesse and thy grace,   Of thy goodness and thy grace,
   For my men and me!'   For my men and me!'

The Gest of Robyn Hode

413 'Yes, for God,' sayd Robyn,
    'And also God me save,
    I aske mercy, my lorde the kynge,
    And for my men I crave.'

414 'Yes, for God,' than sayd our kynge,

    'And therto sent I me,
    With that thou leve the grene wode,

    And all thy company;

415 'And come home, syr, to my courte,
    And there dwell with me.'
    'I make myn avowe to God,' sayd Robyn,

    'And ryght so shall it be.'

416 'I wyll come to your courte,
    Your servyse for to se,
    And brynge with me of my men
    Seven score and thre.

417 'But me lyke well your servyse,
    I **come** agayne full soone
    And shote at the donne dere,
    As I am wonte to done.'

'Yes, for God,' said Robin,
    'And also God me save,
    I ask mercy, my lord the King,
    And for my men I crave.'

'Yes, 'fore God,'
    then said our King,
    'And thereto sent I me,
    With that thou
    leave the greenwood,
    And all thy company;

'And come home, sir, to my court,
    And there dwell with me.'
    'I make mine avowe
    to God,' said Robin,
    'And right so shall it be.

'I will come to your court,
    Your service for to see,
    And bring with me of my men
    Seven score and three.

'But if I like not your service,
    I come again full soon
    And shoot at the dun deer,
    As I am want to done.'

The VIII Fytte **The Eighth Fit**

418 'Haste thou ony grene cloth,' sayd our kynge, 'Hast thou any green cloth,' said our King,
'That thou wylte sell nowe to me?' 'That thou wilt sell now to me?'
'Ye, for God,' sayd Robyn, 'Ye, 'fore God,' said Robin,
'Thyrty yerdes and thre.' 'Thirty yards and three.'

419 'Robyn,' sayd our kynge, 'Robin,' said our King,
'Now pray I the, 'Now pray I thee,
Sell me some of that cloth, Sell me some of that cloth,
To me and my meyne.' To me and my company.'

420 'Yes, for God,' then sayd Robyn, 'Yes, for God,' then said Robin,
'Or elles I were a fole; 'Or else I were a fool;
Another day ye wyll me clothe, Another day ye will me clothe,
I trowe, ayenst the Yole.' I know, against the Yule.'

421 The kynge kest of his cole then, The King cast off his cowl then,
A grene garment he dyde on, A green garment he did on,
And every knyght **had** so, i-wys, And every knight, I know,
Another **had** full sone. Another had full soon.

422 Whan they were clothed in Lyncolne grene, When they were clothed in Lincoln green,
They keste away theyr graye; They cast away their gray;
'Now we shall to Notyngham,' Now we shall to Nottingham,'
All thus our kynge gan say. All thus our King did say.

The Gest of Robyn Hode

423 Theyr **bowes bente**, and forth they went,
    Shotynge all in-fere,
    Towarde the towne of Notyngham,
    Outlawes as they were.

424 Our kynge and Robyn rode togyder,
    For soth as I you say,
    And they shote plucke-buffet,
    As they went by the way.

425 And many a buffet our kynge wan
    Of Robyn Hode that day,
    And nothynge spared good Robyn
    Our kynge in his pay.

426 'So God me helpe,' sayd our kynge,
    'Thy game is nought to lere;
    I shoulde not get a shote of the,
    Though I shote all this yere.'

427 All the people of Notyngham
    They stode and behelde;
    They sawe nothynge but mantels of grene
    That covered all the felde.

Their bowes bent,
and forth they went,
Shooting far and near,
Toward the town of Nottingham,
Outlaws as they were.

Our King and Robin rode together,
For sooth as I you say,
And they shot pluck-buffet,
As they went by the way.

And many a buffet our King won
Of Robin Hood that day,
And nothing spared good Robin
Our King in his pay.

'So God me help,' said our King,
'Thy game is nought to learn;
I should not get a shot of thee,
Though I shot all this year.'

All the people of Nottingham
They stood and beheld;
They saw nothing
but mantles of green
That covered all the field.

428 Than every man to other gan say,
    'I drede our kynge be slone;
    Come Robyn Hode to the towne, i-wys
On lyve he lefte never one.'

Then every man to other did say,
    'I fear our King be slain;
    Come Robin Hood to the town, surely
Of our lives he'll leave not one.'

429 Full hastly they began to fle,
    Both yemen and knaves,
    And olde wyves that myght evyll goo,
They hypped on theyr staves.

Full hastily they began to flee,
    Both yeomen and knaves,
    And old wives that might hardly walk,
They hoppéd on their staves.

430 The kynge loughe full fast,
    And commaunded theym agayne;
    When they se our comly kynge,
    I-wys they were full fayne

The King laughed full fast,
    And commanded them again;
    When they see our comely King,
    Indeed they were full fain.

431 They ete and dranke, and made them glad,

    And sange with notes hye;
    Then bespake our comly kynge
    To Syr Rycharde at the Lee.

They ate and drank, and made them glad,

    And sang with notés high;
    Then bespake our comely King
    To Sir Richard at the Lee.

432 He gave hym there his londe agayne,
    A good man he bad hym be;
    Robyn thanked our comly kynge,
    And set hym on his kne.

He gave him there his land again,
    A good man he bade him be;
    Robin thanked our comely King,
    And set him on his knee.

433 Had Robyn dwelled in kynges courte
   But twelve monethes and thre,
   That he had spent an hondred pounde
   And all his mennes fe.

When Robin had dwelled in the King's court
But twelve months and three,
He had spent a hundred pounds
And all his men's fee.

434 In every place where Robyn came
   Ever more he layde downe,
   Both for knyghtes and for squyres,
   To gete hym grete renowne.

In every place where Robin came
Ever more he laid down,
Both for knights and for squires,
To get him great renown.

435 By than the yere was all agone
   He had no man but twayne,
   Lytell Johan and good Scathelocke,
   With hym all for to gone.

By then the year was past and gone
He had no man but two,
Little John and good Scathelock,
From him the others had gone.

436 Robyn sawe yonge men shote
   Full **ferre** upon a day;
   'Alas!' then sayd good Robyn,
   'My welthe is went away.

Robin saw young men shoot
Full far upon a day;
'Alas!' then said good Robin,
'My wealth is went away.

437 'Somtyme I was an archere good,
   A styffe and eke a stronge;
   I was **comitted** the best archere
   That was in mery Englonde.

'Sometime I was an archer good,
A stout, also a strong;
I was counted the best archer
That was in merry England.'

438 'Alas!' then sayd good Robyn,
   'Alas and well a woo!
   Yf I dwele lenger with the kynge,
   Sorowe wyll me sloo.'

'Alas!' then said good Robin,
'Alas and welladay!
If I dwell longer with the King,
Sorrow will me slay.'

439 Forth than went Robyn Hode
   Tyll he came to our kynge:
   'My lorde the kynge of Englonde,
   Graunte me myn askynge.

440 'I made a chapell in Bernydsale,
   That semely is to se,
   It is of Mary Magdaleyne,
   And thereto wolde I be.

441 'I myght never in this seven nyght
   No tyme to slepe ne wynke,
   Nother all these seven dayes
   Nother ete ne drynke.

442 'Me longeth sore to Bernysdale,
   I may not be therfro;
   Barefote and wolwarde I have hyght

   Thyder for to go.'

443 'Yf it be so,' than sayd our kynge,
   'It may no better be,
   Seven nyght I gyve the leve
   No lengre, to dwell fro me.'

444 'Gramercy, lorde,' then sayd Robyn,
   And set hym on his kne;
   He toke his leve full courteysly,
   To grene wode than went he.

*Forth then went Robin Hood
Till he came to our King:
'My lord the King of England,
Grant me mine asking.

'I made a chapel in Barnsdale,
That seemly is to see,
It is of Mary Magdalene,
And thereto would I be.

'I might never in this seven night
No time to sleep nor wink,
Neither all these seven days
Neither eat nor drink.

'Me longeth sore to Barnsdale,
I may not be therefro';
Barefoot and wool-clad
I have vowed
Thither for to go.'

'If it be so,' than said our King,
'It may no better be,
Seven nights I give the leave —
No longer! — to dwell from me.'

'Gramercy, lord,' then said Robin,
And set him on his knee;
He took his leave full courteously,
To greenwood then went he.*

445 Whan he came to grene wode,
   In a mery mornynge,
   There he herde the notes small
   Of byrdes mery syngynge.

446 'It is ferre gone,' sayd Robyn,
   'That I was last here;
   Me lyste a lytell for to shote
   At the donne dere.'

447 Robyn slewe a full grete harte;
   His horne than gan he blow,
   That all the outlawes of that forest
   That horne coud they knowe.

448 And gadred them togyder,
   In a lytell throwe.
   Seven score of wyght yonge men
   Came redy on a rowe.

449 And fayre dyde of theyr hodes,
   And set them on theyr kne:
   'Welcome,' they sayd, '**our dere** mayster,

   Under this grene-wode tre.'

450 Robyn dwelled in grene wode
   Twenty yere and two;
   For all drede of Edwarde our kynge,
   Agayne wolde he not goo.

When he came to greenwood,
In a merry morning,
There he herd the notés small
Of birds merry singing.

'It is long ago,' said Robin,
'That I was last here;
I lust a little for to shoot
At the dun deer.'

Robin slew a full great hart;
His horn then did he blow,
That all the outlaws of that forest
That horn could they know.

And gathered them together,
As fast as they could go.
Seven score of strong young men
Came ready on a row.

And fair did off their hoods,
And set them on their knee:
'Welcome,' they said,
'our dear master,
Under this greenwood tree.'

Robin dwelled in greenwood
Twenty years and two;
For all dread of Edward our King,
Again would he not go.

451 Yet he was begyled, i-wys, / Yet he was beguiled, I know,
Through a wycked woman, / Through a wicked woman,
The pryoresse of **Kyrkesly***, / The prioress of Kirklees,
That nye was of hys kynne. / That nigh was of his kin.

452 For the love of a knyght, / For the love of a knight,
Syr Roger of **Donkesly**, / Sir Roger of [Doncaster],
That was her owne speciall; / That was her own special;
Full evyll mote they the! / Full evil they did to thee!

453 They toke togyder theyr counsell / They took together their counsel
Robyn Hode for to sle, / Robin Hood for to slay,
And how they myght best do that dede, / And how they might best do that deed,
His banis for to be. / His bane for to be.

454 Than bespake good Robyn, / Than bespoke good Robin,
In place where as he stode, / In place where then he stood,
'To morow I muste to **Kyrkely** / Tomorrow I must to Kirklees
Craftely to be leten blode.' / Skillfully to be leten blood.'

455 Syr Roger of Donkestere, / Sir Roger of Doncaster,
By the pryoresse he lay, / By the prioress he lay,
And there they betrayed good Robyn Hode / And there they betrayed good Robin Hood
Through theyr false playe. / Through their false play.

The Gest of Robyn Hode

456 Cryst have mercy on his soule,   *Christ have mercy on his soul,*
    That dyed on the rode!   *That diéd on the rood!*
    For he was a good outlawe,   *For he was a good outlaw,*
    And dyde pore men moch god.   *And did poor men much good.*

The Text of the Gest

Chances are that we do not have the text of the "Gest" in anything like its original form. The place names it mentions make it almost certain that it was written by a Yorkshireman — and a Yorkshireman who rarely travelled beyond his home county. Yet the text as we have it is in fairly generic Middle English, with few signs of northern dialect. Chaucer could almost have written it; certainly he would have understood it without difficulty. There are Robin Hood ballads in northern dialect, such as "Robin Hood and the Bride," a variant of "Robin Hood and Allen a Dale" [Child 138] found in the Forresters manuscript, but the "Gest" as we have it is not one of them.

And yet, it comes from a time when regional dialects of English were at their strongest and most distinct; "authors in the twelfth, thirteenth, and fourteenth centuries generally wrote the English that they spoke — whether in London, Hereford, Peterborough, or York."[27] The "Gest" is more likely from the fifteenth century. But the expectation would still be that it would contain local linguistic forms.

The lack of Northernisms argues that there was a recensional stage when these characteristics were purged. What's more, because the surviving prints are all in much the same dialect, all our copies must derive from this de-Northernized copy of the text. It has been suggested that "the next move in the investigation of the Robin Hood legend would seem to lie with linguistic scholars."[28] But Lister M. Matheson is the only scholar to study this, and even Matheson's work is very preliminary.

Matheson[29] declares that the printed editions have all adapted the text to fit their preferred dialects, but adds that "a number of Northern spelling and forms survived this process…. Their appearance suggests strongly that the original author was indeed a Northerner and possibly a Yorkshireman." This is a very strong conclusion given his method of comparing the prints against the suggested regional dialects rather than against each other. Still, the conclusion is likely correct.

In any case, because we have only copies, one of our tasks is to try to reconstruct the ancestor of these copies. This is a process known as textual criticism, and what follows is a quite wonkish discussion recommended primarily for specialists.

The Early Copies

Like most of the Robin Hood ballads (and, of course, like the aristocratic romances), we have no field collections of the "Gest" — it is likely that it never existed in tradition. What we have are printed editions. Child's text is based on seven of these, which he calls **a, b, c, d, e, f,** and **g** — a system usually but not always followed by the later scholars. The prints may be briefly described as follows:

a. "A Gest of Robyn Hod," is in the National Library of Scotland. The call number is Advocates Library H.30.a. Discovered in 1785.[30] Often referred to as the "Lettersnijder edition," based on the font used; also sometimes the "Antwerp edition" based on where it is though to have been printed.[31] Contains all or parts of Child's stanzas 1–83, 118–208, 314–349 — just under half the total. Currently consists of leaves 1-5, part of 8, 9-12, and 19-20 of probably 28 original leaves. 33 lines per page. It is Dobson and Taylor's A.

b. "A Lytell Geste of Robyne Hode," printed by Wynkyn de Worde. Complete. Found in the library of the University of Cambridge, Selden 5.18. The earliest complete copy. Dobson and Taylor's B.

c. Bodleian, Douce e.12 (called Fragment #16 by Child). Duff-Bibliog #361. Two leaves. Portions of stanzas 26–60 only, said to have been taken from a binding and to be the central leaves of a quire.[32] Dobson and Taylor refer to Child's **c** and **d** under the siglum D.

d. Bodleian, Douce f.1 (called Fragment #17 by Child). Portions of stanzas 280–350 only. Dobson and Taylor refer to Child's **c** and **d** under the siglum D. The pages were placed in binding strips and have been trimmed; this has resulted in the loss of text at the beginning of lines as well as at the top and bottom of pages. Unusually, this edition indents alternate lines, so that some lines are more defective than others.

e. Bodleian, Douce f.51(3) (called Fragment #16 by Child). Portions of stanzas 435–450 only; from stanza 443 on, only the ends of the lines survive. It is said to have been extracted from a book binding.[33] Dobson/Taylor collectively cite **e**, **p**, and **q** under the symbol P.

f. "A Mery Geste of Robyn Hoode," British Library C.21.c. Printed by William Copland, meaning that it can be dated between 1548 and 1570. Since Copland registered a Robin Hood play in 1560, and since Copland's print contains two dramas as well as the "Gest,"[34] it is likely that 1560 is the year of printing — although Dobson/Taylor suggest that Copland had printed the plays in an earlier separate form, in which case the date must be after 1560. Dobson and Taylor decided to ignore Child's sigla and cite this as C.

g. "A Mery Iest of Robin Hood," Bodleian Library, Z.2.Art.Seld. Printed for Edward White, who was active well into the seventeenth century. It has been suggested on the basis of a Stationer's Register entry that this copy was printed in 1594.[35]

Since Child's time, two more small fragments have been discovered. For reasons having to do with their ownership, I label them **p** and **q** rather than **h** and **i**. They were studied in detail by Oates; the descriptions are from his paper.

- **p.** The "Penrose fragment," formerly owned by Boies Penrose but now in the Folger Shakespeare Library. A full leaf and a portion of a second, recovered from a book binding. Stanzas 227.4–235.2, 243.2–250.4, 312.4–319.3, 327.3–335.1. Dobson and Taylor collectively cite **e**, **p**, and **q** under the symbol P.
- **q.** The University of Cambridge fragment. Found in a book binding and presented to Cambridge University in 1917. Contains 220.1–227.3, 319.4–327.2. Dobson and Taylor collectively cite **e**, **p**, and **q** under the symbol P.

The History of the Prints and Their Relationships

Except for the meagre facts stated above, everything we know about these prints is inference. This information must be gleaned from the typefaces and other obscure hints, and is often highly technical. The results may be found in the section on "The Stemma, or Family Tree, of the Prints." Most important, for textual purposes, is the relationship between **a** and **b** — the only two independent substantial copies.

a — *"Lettersnijder"*: The type of **a** (Lettersnijder) is Lettersnijder 98 — that is, 20 lines are 98 millimeters tall, making the type 13.9 point (in the modern usage of 72 points=1 inch.) The orthography is peculiar. The first page is set entirely as prose — Oates makes the suggestion that it was originally intended to be set as poetry, but then it was decided to include a woodcut of the mounted archer at the top, and the text had to be reset and dramatically compressed to make room for it.[36]

Based on the samples in Isaac,[37] the spaces between words are very small — in a lot of cases, there are no spaces at all. The only punctuation marks are points which are placed almost at random (certainly not where we would place periods; some hardly even qualify as comma breaks) and a handful of section marks, some of which indicate line breaks. It also lacks stanza breaks.

The first letters of lines are capitalized, but in Isaac's first sample, almost nothing else. In the second sample, proper names are often capitalized, as is the pronoun "I." This second section also typically spells "The(e)" with a þ (=th), i.e. y^e or þ^e — a usage not found in the first sample. I suspect that there were two typesetters, one more familiar with English orthography than the other.

Gutch contends that Lettersnijder was issued by Myllar and Chepman in 1508,[38] and Holt also refers to it as among "the Chapman (sic.) and Myllar Prints of 1508."[39]

This is understandable but almost certainly wrong. Chepman and Myllar were authorized to print mass books and other materials in Scotland in 1507, and published for about twenty years.[40] The largest collection of works from their press is Advocates H.30, which also contains the "Gest." This book contains in one binding eleven quarto books. The first nine are typographically similar, and seven of the nine contain a colophon or other markings associating them with Myllar and Chepman. The three with dates are all from 1508: *Porteus of Noblenes*, Chaucer's *The Maying*, and the *Knightly Tale of Gologros and Gawaine*.

The natural assumption is that the last two items in the volume are also from Myllar and Chepman, But every one of the prints certain to have been printed by Myllar and Chepman, according to Isaac, is in a Textura face. The Advocates copy of the "Gest" is not in Textura; it is, of course, in Lettersnijder.

The link to Myllar and Chepman appears dubious on other grounds. All of their works are clearly Scottish. Yet the incipit to the Advocates text of the "Gest" reads "Here begynneth" (English), not "Here begynnis" (Scots),[41] a reading which would surely have been "Scotticised" even if nothing else had been. Thus the strong weight of evidence is that Chepman and Myllar did not print the "Gest." There is, indeed, no reason to think that the printer was Scottish.

Beyond that we can say little, because the Lettersnijder font was common around the beginning of the sixteenth century. Most printers who used Lettersnijder were Dutch, and there are a few instances of errors which make sense in Dutch (e.g. "mijn" for "mine"; 200.3), so it is probable that it was the product of a Dutch press. Lacking knowledge of the printer, the date is uncertain; the period 1510–1520 is often suggested, but it might be a decade or two earlier.

It is clear that compositor did not know English well; he also shows signs of inexperience in his craft. In particular, he seems to have had trouble with inverted letters, such as n/u and, once or twice, m/w. There may also be a few instances of mistaking the letter thorn (þ) for a d when it should have been transcribed th, e.g. in stanza 179. This may indicate that the common ancestor of **a** and **b** still used thorn (þ).

b — *de Worde:* Wynkyn de Worde's **b** text is without doubt the earliest of the complete copies. De Worde (the successor of England's first printer

Caxton) worked from 1492 to 1534. The colophon to **b** has no date but says it was was "Enprented at London: In fletestrete at the sygne of the sone."[42] And de Worde did not move to Fleet Street until 1500. Thus the earliest possible date is in that year.

However, de Worde — although his typography was always behind the times ("most of his printing was of indifferent quality and some of it was thoroughly bad"[43]) — gradually changed his fonts and his library of clip art; he started using nothing but Textura-style blackletter but eventually acquired Roman and Italic and even Greek type[44].

It appears de Worde published the "Gest" using his Textura 95 font. Isaac says that Textura 95 was "the most frequently found of all de Worde's types in the sixteenth century";[45] he used it for his entire career. Duff lists 103 books believe to have been printed by de Worde before 1500; 82 of these use at least some Textura 95, and 26 appear to use it exclusively.[46] However, it did evolve somewhat; in this period, there were multiple forms of the letters a, d, h s, v, w, and y.[47] The heading line of de Worde's edition of the "Gest" uses four of these letters, designated a–1, d–1, h–1, and y–2 by Isaac. The y is datable: de Worde was using y–1 in 1502, but by 1506 had shifted to y–2.[48]

So the date almost has to be after 1503. But on other grounds, the earlier, the better. Binns notes that de Worde printed most of his other romances in the period 1498–1500[49] — e.g. his only four books certainly dated to 1498 the "Description of Britain," the "Morte d'Arthur," the "Canterbury Tales," and the "Legenda Aurea."[50]

The illustration at the head of the **b** print shows a woman, a man carrying a sword backwards, and a man who appears to be a herald. The artwork has no relevance at all to the "Gest," and de Worde gave up a large portion of his clip art, as well as some of his fonts, when he made the move to Fleet Street; much of the material ended up in the hands of another printer, Julian Notary.[51] Had de Worde printed the "Gest" before his move, or long after, he could probably have used better art.

Another argument for a not-too-late date is the fact that, in around 1507, de Worde and his rival Richard Pynson began a policy of cooperation.[52] This ended a strong rivalry that had existed between the two. Given that de Worde and Pynson both seem to have produced editions of the "Gest," this is an argument that both their editions were printed before their agreement.

Based solely on examination of the facsimiles, I thought the date was c. 1505.

Although none of the individual points is decisive, collectively they are strong evidence for Ferguson's date of around 1506;[53] this date is also found in the *Short Title Catalogue of Books Printed in England, Scotland & Ireland, 1475–1640*.[54]

Of all the copies of the "Gest," de Worde's appears to have been the most used. No fewer than three readers put their names in it.[55] One called himself "George Poll" (Powell) and urged readers to kiss his "briche and buttocks." A second simply says "By me John"; this is perhaps John Cony, who signed that name to two other books which were bound with the "Gest," "The assemble of goodes" and "The Frere and the Boye." The third name is entered twice, with different spellings: One claims the book is "Avdary Holman[']s," the other says it is "By me avdery homan of titsey." Audrey Holman also put her name in two of the other books bound with the "Gest." Ohlgren devoted significant effort to trying to locate Audrey Holman, eventually coming up with three candidates,[56] with a likely date toward the end of the sixteenth century. The fact that this copy went through at least three and probably four owners before being entered into the Bagford collection shows how popular it was. This does not, of course, mean that it had a superior text.

c, d — *Fragments*

It is has been stated that **c** and **d** are from the same original. However, even a casual glance at the letter forms shows they are distinct.

Ritson thought **c** to have been printed by Wynkyn de Worde — but dated it 1489.[57] Duff has no doubt that it is by de Worde, noting that "though in the earlier type it has the later I, and Caxton's I does not occur. It cannot be earlier than 1500, and quite probably was printed a year or two later.[58]" Ritson's date is impossible, because de Worde was Caxton's assistant until Caxton died in 1491;[59] de Worde could not produce a book of his own before 1491, and the evidence is that it took him several years to start publishing large numbers of books. Oates, p. 6, accepts the attribution to de Worde, and allows that **c** predates **b**, but does not offer a date.

The type is a slight argument for the attribution to de Worde, but because there are so many Texturas floating around, that's all it is. And, if it is from de Worde, why are there so many differences from **b**? The differences are rarely substantial, but they are numerous.

Farmer instead suggested John Rastell as a printer[60]. Rastell's dates are disputed; Child claims 1517–1536, but Isaac's introduction to Rastell suggests that he was in business from about 1512. However, Rastell is another printer using those ubiquitous Textura types. To me, based on the facsimiles in Isaac, **c** doesn't look like Rastell's style.

Ohlgren suggests that **c** is the work of Hugo Goes of York[61] The connection of **c** with Goes is also found in the *Short Title Catalog*, but the font proves relatively little. We cannot rule out the possibility that Hugo Goes printed the "Gest" — a work which would likely be popular in Yorkshire. But his one known book was in Latin, and the other two whose titles we know also sound like they were intended for clerical use and were in Latin. From such works to the "Gest" is rather a stretch. Since Goes, de Worde, John Scolar, and Thomas Berthelet all had copies of de Worde's Textura 95, and Pynson had something quite close, any of them could have been responsible — indeed, the text looks to me more like the sample of Scolar in Isaac than the sample of Goes. The *Short Title Catalog* suggests 1506–1509 as the date, but with a question mark.

As a specimen of typography, **d** leaves much to be desired. In its few stanzas it manages three times to omit four-line sections (323.3-324.2, 332.3-333.2, 324.1-4). There are other signs of incompetence on the part of the typesetter as well. Probably we should not give great weight to **d**'s readings unless they have support of one of the other prints.

Ohlgren attributed **d** to Julian Notary based on its use of Textura 92,[62] but the difference between Textura 92 and Textura 93 (or even Textura 95) is really only a difference in leading. Ohlgren says Notary was the only "major London printer" to use Textura 92, but offers no reason to think **d** came from a London printer. The *Short Title Catalog* dated it "c. 1515?" — but this was apparently only a guess.

There is another argument against the attribution to Notary, and that is the list of materials Notary printed. The list by Duff contains seven items.[63] Six are in Latin and appear to be church books. The only exception is a print of Chaucer's "Mars and Venus." Notary seems to have been aiming for a rather highbrow market; the "Gest" hardly fits!

It appears that neither **c** nor **d** is directly derived from either **a** or **b**. This means that, where they exist, they are "primary witnesses."

f — *Copland:* Gutch follows Ritson in saying that Copland's **f** print seems to have been derived from **b**,[64] and Clawson declares it "apparently a reprint of **b**."[65] Although "reprint" is too strong a word (the dialect has been modernized and there are some lines have been heavily changed), it is clearly true that **b** is the source; I noticed the matter independently before I saw the claim in Gutch. It is strange to note that Child and other recent editors seem to have paid little attention to this fact — Child cites the variants in **f** without saying anything about the ancestry of that print. (He did note in his very short introduction to the "Gest" in Child-ESB that **f** is "apparently made" from **b**, but does not pursue the fact.)

It is hardly surprising that William Copland followed the text of de Worde. It is believed that William Copland was either the younger brother or the son of another printer, Robert Copland — and Copland the elder actually worked for Wynkyn de Worde early in his career.[66] Robert Copland apparently was responsible for editing some of de Worde's editions;[67] he was also mentioned in de Worde's will.[68]

Thus it is very likely that William Copland would have worked from a copy of de Worde's own earlier printing — indeed, it is possible that Robert Copland worked on **b**. Ohlgren suggests that the "rose garland" used in the archery contest of stanza 398 may have been an interpolation by Copland.[69] The difficulty with this is, if Copland had been rewriting the "Gest," why didn't he fill in the several lacunae in the poem? And we find other mentions of rose garlands in the Robin Hood literature.[70]

g — *White:* White's **g** text rarely gets much attention, simply because it is so much later than the others. It is instantly clear that the text has been much modernized, although this does not prove whether it is from a good or a bad source. We will cover its affinities below.

e, p, q — *Fragments of a single edition*: From the pagination and lineation, it is evident that the two fragments **p** and **q** are from the same edition. It is also widely believed that **e** is part of the same print (although not necessarily part of the same copy of that print). It is also clear from the fact that the first verses of **q** come before the first verses of **p**, but the last verses of **p** come before the last verses of **q**, that the two were not properly bound in a single quire. Oates is convinced that they were mis-collated — that is, the edition had its pages out of order.[71]

This raises an interesting point. The **epq** text is widely attributed to Richard Pynson. The suggestion seems to go back to Duff, based on a single leaf of **q** (even though he admits that the "collation [is] not known"),[72] was affirmed by Isaac,[73] and was accepted without question by Oates,[74] Dobson/Taylor,[75] and Ohlgren.[76] In terms of the type, this fits — **epq** seems to be in the Textura 95 that Isaac says was Pynson's standard type.[77]

But almost everyone had a Textura 95: de Worde,[78] Pynson (indeed Pynson's collection of ornaments includes several which appear to me to be exactly the same as those de Worde used in the "Gest")[79], Hugo Goes (Goes acquired his Textura from de Worde),[80] Robert Copland,[81] John Scolar (he and his successor Charles Kyrfoth, like Goes, had their Textura from de Worde),[82] John Skot,[83] Thomas Berthelet (Isaac says that this is another instance where that printer acquired it from de Worde),[84] John

Byddell (yet another who had worked for de Worde and may have gotten some of his type),[85] and John Herford.[86]

> Ome to me sayth our mercyfull lorde / all that labo⸗
> reth and be chargeb / and I shall gyue vnto you refre⸗
> cyon. And the brede that I shall gyue vnto you: shalbe my

abcdefghiklmnop rſstuw p Pynson's Textura

abcdefghiklmnop rſstuw p de Worde's Textura

> A Man may shewe.xii.fruytes cometh / and
> procedeth of trewe penaunce. The fyrst is
> illumynacyon of the soule for thre thynges / fyrste

The Textura 95 Types of Richard Pynson and Wynkyn de Worde
Top: from Pynson's 1504 edition of *The Imitation of Christ*.
Bottom: from de Worde's 1502 *The Ordinary of Christianity*.... The two are not identical; compare the letters d, h, m, o, ſ, w, and y. Differences in type need not indicate a different printer; De Worde had twelve different forms of w, four of h and s, three of u/v and y, two of a and d.

In addition Julian Notary had a Textura 92,[87] as did Ursin Mylner.[88] There were Textura 93s in the library of John Rastell,[89] Henry Pepwell,[90] Peter Treveris,[91] and Richard Bankes.[92] Even Chepman and Myllar, in Scotland, used a Textura 93 similar to de Worde's Textura 95.[93] Moreover, as Duff points out, "it is clear that almost all early English printers well understood what is now called 'leading,' that is, producing a greater space between the lines by inserting slips of metal, so that we find the same type often with two, sometimes with three, different measurements."[94] Thus simply measuring the height of the type is not sufficient to determine which font it is.

The Gest of Robyn Hode

Ohlgren says that **epq** uses the forms of w and s found in Pynson's Textura 95.[95] This appears to be correct, but the sample is small. The fact that **epq** seems to be in Pynson's type is not proof. Matheson affirms that the orthography of **epq** matches Pynson's.[96] This too is strong evidence at a time when printers followed very different standards. But it appears from that Matheson used only a small collection of facsimiles,[97] meaning he didn't have much material to work with.

Pynson's work was noteworthy. "Pynson published some 400 books, technically and typographically the best of the English incunabula."[98]

> Pynson was without doubt the finest printer of his day. He had a fine range of types and used them well. His press-work was superior to that of his contemporaries. He used illustration more sparingly and more effectively than de Worde, and was much more successful with his decorative initials and borders.[99]

Yet he decided to print something completely different in the "Gest,' and when he did so, he got the pages in the wrong order?

The matter is trivial; we are less concerned with the printer of **epq** than its text, but I do think caution is indicated. The one important result of Ohlgren's examination is that, if **epq** is indeed by Pynson (and I think it likely, just not certain), then it almost certainly dates from 1505 or earlier, when Pynson adopted a different form of **w**.

There is agreement that all these prints have a recent common source, possibly a lost printed copy but more probably (given the dates of Pynson and de Worde) a manuscript, and clearly not the original, since all copies share certain defects. Further evidence for a recent source is shown by the fact that all the copies are relatively similar.

Comparing the Texts: Printers, Dates, and Ancestry

Turning to the relationship between these prints, Dobson/Taylor suggest that **a** is "apparently a cheap reprint of a previous and now lost edition by Richard Pynson,"[100] that is, of **epq**. This follows from a comparison made by Oates,, who compared the 70 lines for which **epq** and **a** both survive.[101] Oates found several significant differences between **a** and **epq**, but six times as many cases where the two agree with each other against **b**. It is clear that they represent a single phase of the text, and it is likely that one is a copy of the other.

Oates is convinced that **a** is a copy of **epq**. And his evidence extends beyond the textual. The woodcut at the head of the Lettersnijder edition is a copy of one used by Pynson in his edition of the *Canterbury Tales*. But it is certainly a copy — the images can be seen side by side on pp. 104–105 of Ohlgren/Matheson, and the Canterbury version differs in the face, the spurs, the ribbons on the horse, and other details from the Lettersnijder version; in addition, Lettersnijder is cropped more closely. Oates believes — and I think it almost certain he is correct — that Pynson used that same illustration in his edition of the "Gest" as he did in the *Tales*, and the Lettersnijder printer then copied it.

Matheson seems to confirm Oates's conclusions on other grounds, declaring on that the spelling of **a** closely matches **epq**.[102] He does note a few variants in **a** which are valid English alternatives rather than errors, and suggests that this might mean that a native English speaker was involved in the typesetting of **a**. Alternately, the copy of **epq** used to

The Gest of Robyn Hode 121

create **a** had a few corrections written into it — or perhaps these variants are from the typesetter who knew English, as opposed to the one (responsible for the majority of the remaining text) who did not.

There is a secondary point: If the Lettersnijder edition is derived from Pynson, it must be post–1490, when Pynson began printing, and likely post–1495. If Duff is correct in dating Pynson to 1500, then a date after 1510 seems likely for Lettersnijder — which likely makes it more recent than de Worde's print. (On the other hand, Ohlgren suggests a date in the early 1490s for Pynson,[103] which lets Ohlgren claim a date of *c.* 1495 for Lettersnijder.[104])

Looking at the other substantial copies, it is instantly clear that **f** and **g** go together — **g** looks like a modernized copy of **f**, perhaps compared with a partial copy of **b**; most of the differences between **f** and **g** are cases of an archaic form in **f** being replaced by a more modern form in g. Clawson calls it "very similar" to **f**.[105] Phillips/Keatman call it a "second generation" copy of **b**,[106] without mentioning that **f** is the intermediate generation — but there really isn't much doubt.

I would be inclined to date **g** as late as possible — a Jacobean date would be far better than an Elizabethan, and frankly, I'm inclined to suspect that the attribution to White is deceptive and the piece was actually printed in the reign of Charles I. **f** also has some signs of modernization, although far fewer than **g**.

It is also clear that **f** and **g** go with **b**. The relationship between **b** and **f** is noted by Ohlgren with the observation that **f** has had its language modernized.[107] Ohlgren suggests that Copland printed the work in part because of its anti-clerical tone.[108]

There are strong indications that the copy of **b** used by the compositor of **f** was damaged. A good example is in stanza 305. The text of **b** has Little John say "No lyfe on me be lefte." All **fg** can offer is "That after I eate no bread," which is so utterly feeble that the only possible explanation is that the source was damaged. In stanza 400, **b** has "And bere a buffet on his hede, I-wys right al bare," while **fg** give us "A good buffet on his head bare, For that shal be his fine," which fails to rhyme and is inept anyway. These readings suffice to prove the kinship of **fg**.

Child does seem to have realized that **fg** were relatives of **b**, but he does not really describe the situation, if indeed he even thought in terms of a stemma. But it seems clear that we have two basic groups, which we might call Pynson and de Worde. Pynson consists of **epq** and **a**, with **a** having value only where **epq** is defective (admittedly, more than 80% of our knowledge of the Pynson text comes from **a**). de Worde consists of **bfg** — and, because **b** is complete, this means not only that **g** has no value (as was recognized, e.g. by Dobson/Taylor and Ohlgren) but *also that f has no value.*

Unfortunately, the fragments **c** and **d** are both so short that their affinities cannot be firmly established. My feeling is that **c** and **d** are closer to the **b** group than to **a**, but not as close to **b** as are **fg**. This conflicts with the opinion of Ohlgren, who thinks (on the basis of spelling rather than text) that **c** is another copy of Pynson.[109] But if that is the case, why is it so distinct from **a**? The best guess is that it is independent.

Where the fragments **c d** are extant, they can give us some help. But the two combined include less than a quarter of the "Gest." For the

The Gest of Robyn Hode   123

largest part of the poem, we are stuck choosing between **a** and **b** — or, indeed, between **b** and conjectural emendation.

Although we cannot prove whether **epq/a** or **b** is the older text, Child,[110] Dobson/Taylor, and Knight/Ohlgren[111] all consider **a** to be the more primitive — but Child's evidence is summarized in a single note listing about a dozen variants. The primary evidence, really, is that **a** was incompetently typeset (note that there is a *homoioteleuton* error as early as the second stanza), meaning that the typesetter probably was not making deliberate changes. Child in particular takes **a** as his copy text insofar as it is extant; he uses other readings only where it appears badly corrupt. Both Child and Knight/Ohlgren follow their copy text so closely as to alternate between spelling Little John's name "Lytel" where **b** is the copy text and "Litell" where **a** is extant — an obvious absurdity (although I do it too in that case). Ohlgren later pulled back somewhat:

> Since 1899.... all of the poem's editors have repeated Child's assertion that the Lettersnijder edition [**a**].... is the earliest surviving edition.... and hence it has been given pride of place in various critical editions, even though it is in an incomplete state. It has even supplanted the almost-complete Wynkyn de Worde edition [**b**].[112]

This even though, as Ohlgren continues, "Lettersnijder is not only a decidedly poorer version of the text but also an almost incompetent copy of an earlier version by Richard Pynson, which now must be recognized as the earliest surviving edition of the poem."

It is at this point that the fact that the text we have is not in a northern dialect becomes important. The common ancestor of **a** and **b** was not the original — and if **a** preserves this edited text better than **b**, that *doesn't make it significantly closer to the original.*

Hence I think Child's extreme preference for **a** exaggerated. True, it has older grammatical forms. But recall that it is probably Dutch, typeset by a Dutch compositor. Many of its errors are pure and simple goofs — e.g. in 6.4, "vnkoutg" for "vnkouth"; 15.4 "mynge" for "mynde." Clearly the compositor of **a** simply transcribed the original mechanically.

Wynkyn de Worde, although born in the Low Countries, was thoroughly familiar with English, and his work was designed to make English audiences comfortable — and, indeed, to standardize the language. His press made a habit of updating grammatical forms.[113] His text of the "Gest" has surely been touched up, so if the question is solely one of grammatical form, **a** is generally to be preferred. But there is no hint that de Worde made substantial revisions. Where the difference is one of fundamental meaning, as opposed to grammatical form, **b** has as much authority as **a**, and the poem should be re-edited on that basis.

The fact that Pynson and de Worde and (apparently) three other printers all issued versions of the "Gest" around the beginning of the fifteenth century is obviously a testimony to its popularity. But the fact that Pynson and de Worde have noticeably different texts is also noteworthy. If two printers, who sometimes worked together and were for very long based on the same street, produced substantially different versions, this clearly implies that one is not dependent on the other.

Bottom line: The text of the "Gest" needs to be re-edited eclectically, based on the Pynson and de Worde types, with **c** and **d** consulted where extant and conjectural emendation used where necessary, especially in the places where Pynson is lost.

The Gest of Robyn Hode

Fortunately relatively few of the differences between the texts are major — the main reason why the texts are considered to go back to a single fairly recent original. But at least one variant, in Stanza 53, is potentially significant;.

If we were to grade the condition of the text, we would probably list it as "fair." There is no real doubt as to the general course of the narrative, meaning that the text of the "Gest" is in better shape than, say, the text of "Robin Hood's Death." But the amount of minor damage is extensive. As a result, I have included a textual commentary to discuss some of the more meaningful variants.

Based on the similarity between the surviving texts, the archetype of the surviving versions (that is, their most recent common ancestor) probably dates from the reign of Henry VI or Edward IV (i.e. between 1422 and 1483), with the latter reign more likely than the former; this is obviously the latest possible date of composition. But it is nearly certain that there were several generations of copies between the poet's autograph manuscript and the last common ancestor of our surviving copies. The various common errors, such as the lost first line of Stanza 7, demonstrate this.

The Stemma, or Family Tree, of the Prints

All of the above allows us to construct a "stemma," or family tree, of the "Gest," and to edit the poem on stemmatic principles — a method not used by any previous editor. A reconstruction of some sort is necessary because all we have are several late prints. Child's was the first real attempt to collate and edit the text to create a critical edition — that is, one which compared the prints to try to determine the original they pointed to. Child had most of the materials available to us (the only new discoveries since his time are the fragments **p** and **q**), but his approach was based on treating **a** as his main source — the "copy text" method. The historical evidence does not seem to support this. This document is an attempt to reconstruct the "Gest" based on stemmatic methods in the light of more recent research.

The stemma used in this reconstruction is as follows:

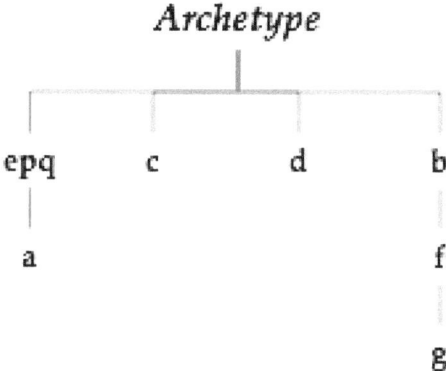

The Stemma of the Prints of the "Gest"

The "Archetype" is the most recent common ancestor of all our existing copies. In this case, it clearly is not the original, because of the defects common in all the existing prints (the loss of line 7.1, etc.). But it is the earliest copy to which we have actual testimony. We then try to guess at what came the true original said. The methods used are largely those developed two centuries ago by Karl Lachmann, and covered in most manuals of textual criticism; I will not summarize them here.

We have four "primary" copies of the archetype — that is, copies which derive from it with no *surviving* intermediate copies. These four copies are the complete edition **b** and the fragmentary copies **c d epq**.

The substantial fragment **a** is a very poor copy of **epq**; the complete copy **f** is derived from **b**; the complete copy **g** is derived from **f** (with perhaps some comparison with **b** in the early stanzas).

The diagram below gives a rough outline of the surviving contents of each of the prints. It shows ten-stanza blocks and whether each text is complete (•), partial (o), or lacking entirely( ). The line at the top shows the stanza numbers, in blocks of 50.

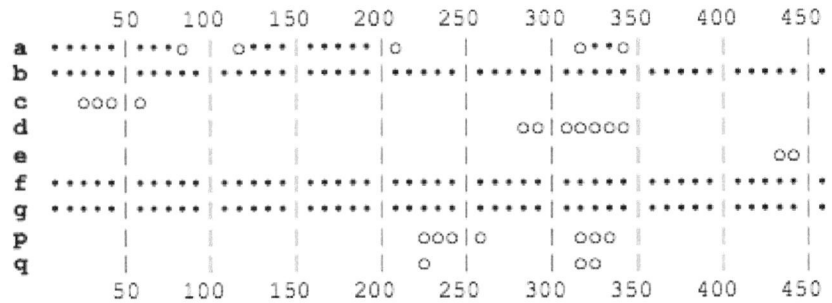

The Extent of the Prints of the "Gest"

Thus for about half the text we have only one substantial independent witness (**b**); in these places we have little option but to try to parse the text and emend it where it does not make sense. For the rest, we have two witnesses (usually **a** and **b**), and we compare them to try to find the original.

Notes on the Text of the "Gest"

As mentioned in the Introduction, there are very many variants among the prints of the "Gest," and some places where the text has been entirely lost. Many scholars have worked on the text, but none of the editions — including this one — can be considered the last word. This section gives information about some of the most important variants and their meanings, as well as the sources of the readings. A fuller list of variants, with critical apparatus, can be found in the larger volume. The prints are referred to by Child's sigla, **a b c d e f g** (plus **p q** for the fragments found since his time). For discussion of these copies, see the section "The Text of the Gest."

Stanza 4.1; also stanzas 17, 61, 68, 74, 77, 83, 208, 293, 402, 435.

"Scarlock/Scathelock" is a variant we meet several times. The **a** text, where it exists, calls this character "Scarlock," while **b** and **f** use "Scathelock," which **g** simplifies to "Scathlock." The fragment **d** has "Scathelock" in stanza 293, which is perhaps as close as we can come to a "tiebreaker." All the previous editions have used "Scarlock" where **a** exists, "Scathelock" elsewhere. For reasons explained in the introduction, this edition uses "Scathelock" consistently.

This is an interesting case of the tradition being initially rather confused, then settling down on the reading "Scarlet(t)." If we turn to the other ballads, "Guy of Gisborne," stanza 13, refers to "Scarlett"; the "Monk" has "Wyll Scathlok" in stanza 63, and the Percy text of the "Death" has "Will Scarlett" in stanza 2. The parliamentary roll for Winchester in 1432 has the gag line "Robyn, hode, Inne, Grenewode, Stode, Godeman, was, hee, lytel Joon, Muchette Millerson, Scathelock, Reynold."[114] We find other names in the later ballads, e.g. the first line of "Robin Hood and the Prince of Aragon" [Child 129] calls him "Will Scadlock." The Forresters manuscript version of "Robin Hood's Delight" [Child 136] corrects the "Scarlock" of the broadsides to "Scathlock."[115] There is also an instance in the Forresters book where a later hand has corrected "Will Stutley" to "Will Scathlock" in the title of the ballad "Robin Hood Rescuing Will Stutly" [Child 141],[116] but the manuscript also uses "Scarlett" and (once) "Scarett."

The modern preference for "Scarlet" may be the result of Shakespeare, who in 2 *Henry IV,* V.iii, line 103, has Silence sing "And Robin Hood, Scarlet, and John." (This is one of three instances of Shakespeare mentioning Robin Hood; none of the mentions is substantial enough to tell us anything.)

Stanza 7.1: The line that begins Stanza 7 is lacking in all texts; Child prints it as a lacuna. Knight/Ohlgren offer the conjecture "Here shal come a lord or sire." This rhymes with the third line of the stanza — but the first and third lines do not normally rhyme in the "Gest."

Dobson and Taylor's conjecture is "Till that I have som bolde baron," which is rather better but doesn't seem to fit Robin's preoccupations. I doubt we can conjecture the original, but my thought (arrived at without seeing Dobson/Taylor) is, "We shal wait (i.e. await) som bold abbot."

Stanza 53.1: This variant is discussed in the preface; **bf** read "Lancastshyre," **a** has "Lancaster," followed by the editions of Child, Dobson/Taylor, and Knight/Ohlgren; **c** gives us "Lancasesshyre"; and Gummere accepted the reading "Lancashire" found in **g**. Presumably, Child followed **a** on the basis that he always followed **a**. But the reading which best explains the others is surely "Lancastshyre," as in **b**; anyone confronted with this reading would either convert it to "Lancashire" (as **g** did) or simplify it to "Lancaster." This potentially changes the significance of the text, because "Lancashire" is quite definitely a place reference — but "Lancaster" is, potentially at least, a political reference. If the poem in its final form dates from the Wars of the Roses era, it might be a reference to the House of Lancaster and the followers of King Henry VI. If the roots go back to the time of Edward II, it is an even more interesting reference, because Edward II's great enemy was his cousin Thomas Earl of Lancaster. If the knight's son slew a supporter of Lancaster, then this might be a statement that he is a member of the King's party rather than Lancaster's party....

Stanza 76.4: All the editions follow Child in reading this line "God graunt that he [the knight] be true," which is the reading of **a**. But **b** has the very interesting reading "leve" instead of "graunt." "Leve" is short for "believe," i.e. "trust." This is difficult enough that **fg** emend it to "lende." But, while difficult, it is not impossible. It is easy to see how "leve" could be replaced by "graunt," difficult to see how the reverse could come about. I might also conjecture that the original was "give." The variant involves a very different sense. If the original reads "graunte," then this is a simple prayer. But if the reading is "leve," then Robin is making a statement of faith about the knight — rather odd, in light of his later doubts.

Stanza 87.1: All the extant texts (**bfg**) omit this line. Child suggested duplicating it from the previous stanza, on the ground that it might have fallen out because the two lines have the same ending (*homoioteleuton*). This reasonable emendation is adopted by the more recent editors, with minor variations, but is beyond proof. I would be more inclined to a reading with the sense "He borowed it a yere ago."

Stanza 89.2: The text of this part of the poem is troubled. Corruption is probable in stanza 88; it is almost certain in the second line of 89. Child and Gummere both read "In Englonde is his [the knight's] right," following **fg**. But **b**'s reading, followed by Dobson/Taylor, is "In Englonde he is ryght." If the **fg** reading were original, there would be no reason for the other reading to arise. Knight/Ohlgren emend by omitting the words. This text follows **b** on the grounds that only it explains the others. And there is an interesting twist: The Church forbade usurious loans — except that Crusaders were allowed to take them because it was the only way they could quickly gain the money needed for the crusade.[117] In return, the Crusader's property was to be protected until he came home. The reading is perhaps to be understood as meaning that his property in England is to be guarded — the abbot has no right to the land while the knight is away.

Stanza 93.3: This is one of the more significant textual problems of the "Gest." Child's text refers to the "hye justyce" of England — but this reading is supported only by **f(g)**. The only other extant witness, **b**, omits the word "hye." Presumably Child includes the word because it makes no sense to refer to one man as "the justice of England." And the phrase "hye justice" is found without variants in stanza 266. On the other hand, there was no office of "high justice of England" at this time. Possibly "high" is just a word the poet uses to fill a syllable before an office. Still, it is a strange reading, and it seems better to omit the word "hye." Another possibility, which I have not seen elsewhere but which I almost adopted, is to emend "Englonde" rather than "justice." All our problems would disappear if the text read something like "the justice of the foreste" — we know exactly what office that was!

Stanza 98.1: The line is missing in all witnesses. Child conjectured the text "They put on their symple wedes" based on the third line of the previous stanza. The probability is high that more than one line is damaged; the previous stanza does not fit with what has gone before. Instead of inserting a line here, an alternate proposal might be to omit the last three lines of stanza 97 and combine it with the last three lines of 98, or something similar. So possible readings would be something like

Than bespake that gentyll knyght, And with him Lytell Johnn, The porter was redy hymselfe, And welcomed them euerychone (emending the second line), or

Than arrived that gentyll knyght, They came to the gates anone; The porter was redy hymselfe, And welcomed them euerychone (emending the first line).

Stanza 126.4: The knight's home is listed as "Verysdale," with no variation in the prints, but no such place is known. Ritson declared that there was a Lancashire forest named "Wierysdale."[118] I'm more tempted by "Weardale," the region along the Wear in Durham. The usual suggestion, however, is that Verysdale is Lee in Wyresdale.[119] The Wyre river is in Lancashire, somewhat north of the Ribble; Lee is not far from the town of Lancaster, being somewhat to the south and east at the crossing of the Wyre. This fits with the statement in Stanza 53 that the knight's son slew a Lancashire/Lancaster knight; presumably the boy killed someone close to home. The emendation most tempting to me, however, is "Ayredale" — an error of copying rather than of hearing. The river Aire flows east into the Ouse between York and Doncaster. Indeed, Ferrybridge over the Aire is on the Great North Road. In other words, it is right on the knight's path. This would fit well with the situation in Stanza 310.

Stanza 135.1-135A.4: This stanza is surely corrupt. Child gives 135.1 in full as "But as he went at a brydge ther was a wrastelyng," which is too long and rather nonsensical. Child suggests "at Wentbrydge" as an emendation for "Went at a brydge." This seems logical, since the place near Barnsdale where Watling Street crosses the Went is called, unsurprisingly, "Wentbridge," but it is still too long. My suspicion is that what we have is a case of three lines being lost. The text "But as he went at a brydge ther was a wrastelyng" is actually two lines, with the final two lines of that stanza, and the first line of the next stanza, missing. This is the way I have printed the text. I have also conjectured three possible missing lines. I do not in fact think it at all likely that the conjectures are correct, but I used them to fill out the modernized version of the text.

Stanza 186.1: Child's plural "their tyndes" (points of the antlers), the reading of **a**, points to the antlers of the entire herd of deer John is describing; **b**'s "his tynde" reading refers presumably to the green hart (i.e. Robin Hood) at their head. It is awkward to see the antlers referred to in the singular, but if they *were* spoken of as singular, it would invite correction. There is much to be said for the **b** reading — it is an even sharper hint to the Sheriff than the **a** reading.

Stanza 248.3: All the critical editions read that the monk is true, following **bfg**. This has a sharply ironic point: The monk is true not in his statement that he had twenty marks but in being the bearer of the Virgin's repayment of Robin. In other words, it it really Mary who is true. But **p**, which came to light after Child and Gummere published their editions, has the fascinating reading that the *knight* is true. It is very hard to choose between these readings; the reading referring to the knight might be original — with John criticizing Robin for not trusting the knight. Some commentators have seen a running conflict between Robin and John in this section; if so, the **p** reading probably supports their contention.

Stanza 268.1-268A.2: "'But take not a grefe,' sayde the knyght, 'That I heve been so longe... '" This is the first line of stanza 268 as printed by Child, on the evidence of **b**. **f** prints it as two lines — both of them metrically correct — making up the line count by combining the last two lines of 270. The line as given by **b** is patently too long, as the compositor of **f** recognized. Knight/Ohlgren seek to emend by taking out "sayde the knyght." That emendation is required is clear, but this leaves a line still too long, and there is no reason for this. I suspect that this is another instance where we have three missing lines. We may also see evidence of this in the first line of 270, which like the first line of 268 is badly overburdened. The original reading was perhaps something like this:

268. 'But take not a grefe,' sayde the knyght,

'That I have been so long.

For as I came to grene wode

I stopped to rite a wrong. (Or "I met a yeman strong," or some such).

268A. 'For as I passed Wentesbridg

I came by wrastelyng...'

This is an entirely tentative reconstruction, which I strongly doubt matches the original, but we should at least mark that the text is corrupt.

Stanza 315.3: Child's text says that the knight will maintain Robin for "forty" days based on the reading "xl" of **a**, but **b** reads "twelve."

And the two are easily confused in a lot of scripts, since forty is "xl" and twelve is "xii." But there are just too many Biblical uses of the phrase "forty days," plus forty days was the standard period of sanctuary in a church.[120] A scribe might naturally think of forty days when thinking of the knight giving sanctuary. The reading "twelve" is an indication that this is not sanctuary, it is a freely-given promise.

Stanzas 338.4-339.1: Child leaves blank the last line of stanza 338 and the first stanza of 339, which are lacking in all three of the best witnesses, **abd**. **fg** have, with minor variations, "The proude shirife than sayd he" for the last line of 338 but omit the second line of 339, leaving a two-line fragment. Knight/Ohlgren accept the **f** reading in stanza 338 (since it almost certainly mentioned the sheriff, and had to rhyme with "the"). In stanza 339, they repeat this with a variant, which is possible, but at least two other types of emendation are equally possible, along the lines of: "They taken hym to Nottyngham" (referring to his destination) or "They took him but two hours past" (referring to the time). The sense is almost certainly similar to what I offer in the modernized parallel: "And where may he now be?" in 338 and "The Sheriff hath my lord taken" in 339.

Stanza 343.2: The text of Child, following **ad**, says that Robin wishes to see and take (i.e. capture) the Sheriff. This implies a desire for revenge. But **bfg** say that Robin wishes to see and take (i.e. rescue) the knight. This is more a case of fulfilling a duty, and perhaps says more about Robin's honor. Both readings have substantial merit. Since there is no real reason to prefer one over the other, we should probably follow **ad** over **b**.

Stanza 351.2: In this stanza Robin cuts.... something.... in two to free the knight. What was it? **b** says his "hoode." Child emends this to "bonde," which certainly Robin must have cut at some point and is in any case a better rhyme. Knight/Ohlgren note on p. 163 that in stanza 332 the knight was merely bound hand and foot,[121] not hooded. Nonetheless the **b** reading could have been correct; the guards could have tied the knight's hood over his eyes to prevent him from seeing. It is the harder reading, and the author might have used it to insult the sheriff: not only did he bind the knight, he wouldn't even let him see. Another possibility might be to emend to "hondes," i.e. Robin cut in two the ropes binding his hands.

Stanza 377.4: The line Child prints here, "Other shyft have not wee," is lacking in **b**; he takes it from **fg**. **b** instead repeats the text of the second line of the stanza, "Under the grene-wode tre." Knight/Ohlgren, p. 166, accept that the poet meant to repeat the line, but he could surely have produced some sort of change. The fourth line is probably lost forever; we must either conjecture it or accept the **fg** reading, itself surely a conjecture although one of the few conjectures by **f** that is competent. An alternate emendation might be something like "My mynie and me" or "My mery men and me," or perhaps "No other property/land have we." This emphasizes the fact that Robin and his men seem to have no history or place outside the greenwood.

Stanza 381.4: Child's text is "I wolde vouch it safe on the." The reading of **b** is, however, "I vouch it half on the." This confused **f** enough that it read "I would give it to thee." The reading of **b** is indeed strange and possibly corrupt, but Child's emendation does not explain how it came to be corrupt. Child's reading seems to make Robin a banker —

something we do not see elsewhere. The reading of **b** may be an indication that Robin's fame is growing: visitors know the fee they will have to pay, and are prepared to give it.

Stanza 385.1-2: The reading of the first line is a crux. The text of **b** says that the king showed his broad "tarpe." There seems to be no such word in Middle English. Certainly it confused the compositors of **fg**, who change it to "seale." Child, who was more facile with an emendation, instead proposed "targe," followed by most modern editors — but this is not a great help. A reading such as "charter" or "letter" would fit better, but it is harder to explain the error of **b** in that case. A possible suggestion would be to emend the second line of 385, replacing "sone" with "seale." Then the "targe" becomes a letter showing the king's shield (so it can be seen at a distance) and sealed with his seal (for detailed examination). Certainly the outlaws must have seen the seal at some point in the process. Possibly this would even be how they recognized the king in Stanza 411?

Stanza 412.1: Child had two versions of this line. In his original edition, he followed **b** and printed

'Mercy then, Robyn,' sayd our kynge.'

In a correction (volume V., p. 297 in the Dover edition) he amended this to follow **fg**:

'Mercy,' then said Robyn to our kynge.'

Clearly the compositor of **f** was bothered by this reading — which he may not have been able to read clearly; there are signs his original was damaged at this point. He probably didn't like the fact that it made the King show fear, and corrected it to make it appear that Robin, not the King, is asking mercy.

Stanzas 451.3, 454.3: The place where Robin Hood was killed is somewhat uncertain. Child prints "Kyrkesly" in stanza 451, "Kyrke[s]ly" in 454; **bfg** all read Kyrkesly in the first and Kyrkesly in the second. In the "A" (Percy folio) text of the "Death," it is "Churchles" or "Churchlees," which is a less northern version of "Kirk-Lee." The broadside versions of the "Death" (Child's "B") give "Kirkly" or "Kirkly-Hall," which is also the reading of the Davis text from Virginia. The retelling of this tale in "Robin Hood and the Valiant Knight" [Child 153] has a tail note which reads "Birkslay," perhaps derived from the reading "Bircklies" printed by Grafton.

The region of Kirklees on modern maps is south and somewhat west of Leeds, northeast of Manchester, and west of Wakefield. Knight/Ohlgren, p. 168, following Child, point specifically to the priory of Kirklees in west Yorkshire. This is presumably the place intended; the original reading of the text here is anyone's guess.

Divergences from Child's text of the "Gest"

Note: The following list counts only substantial differences; it does not include where the Child text has [brackets] but otherwise agrees with the text above. There are a total of 126 variants between the two texts.

The list below shows the verse and line number and the text chosen by Child; one may refer to the text above to see my preferred reading.

4.1 Scarlok • **5.3** and ye • **7.3** som • **9.3** *omit* was • **11.4** that we • **13.4** tilleth • **14.4** wol • **17.3** Scarlok • **18.3** unkuth • **21.1** in to • **32.2** to • **36.2** it have • **38.3** Lyttel • **40.1** hast • **41.4** No • **43.3** tidynges • **45.3** warte • **50.2** shaped

51.1 than sayde • **51.4** kynd[e]nesse • **53.1** Lancaster • **56.2** woll • **57.4** no • **61.2** Scarlok • **61.2** Muche in • **62.2** frende • **62.2** borowe • **62.2** wolde • **62.4** on tree • **63.3** wolde • **68.2** Scarlok • **68.4** eight and twenty

The Gest of Robyn Hode

• **70.4** lappe • **73.1** at every • **74.1** Scarlok • **75.3** a hors • **75.4** home this • **76.4** graunt • **77.3** Scarlok • **78.2** clene • **83.2** Scarlok • **87.1** He borowed foure hondred pounde • **89.2** is his • **93.3** [hye] justyce • **94.2** theyr • **98.1** They put on their symple wedes

128.3 had be • **135.1-2** *(print as one line)* • **135A** *(combine with 135)* • **137.2** *omit* good • **139.2** where he

155.1 fell • **156.4** me my dynere • **157.4** gif • **160.2** went near • **160.3** ier • **165.3** to God • **166.1** and hardy • **170.4** chaunged • **175.4** thei not • **178.1** *omit* And • **179.2** sendeth the • **185.1** sawe • **188.3** before • **191.3** sawe • **192.4** I graunt • **193.3** commaunde[d] • **195.3** shulde lye • **196.1** lay the

201.3 best[e] • **204.1** hathe • **208.3** Scarlok • **209.3** some • **213.1** they • **214.4** these • **215.2** your • **216.1** [men] • **228.1** *omit* than • **228.2** *omit* nowe • **249.2** what

268A *(combine with 268)* • **271.3** [hye] selerer • **280.2** his • **283.3** allther • **284.1** allther • **290.2** he[ve]de • **291.3** proud[e] • **292.2** he • **300.3** proud[e]

303.2 love[d]st • **312.1** moche I • **313.3** proud[e] • **314.4** walles • **315.3** forty dayes • **319.3** enemys • **319.4** lawe • **320.2** that here • **324.3** wyll be • **326.1** Go nowe home, shyref, sayde our kynge • **329.4** Thereof • **331.1** the gentyll • **332.3** *omit* home • **336.3** Ladyes sake • **337.1** *omit* never • **337.3** bowne • **338.2** so free • **340.3** mery men • **343.4** I-quyte then • **346.2** this fast

352.1 bonde • **356.2** understode • **368.3** by yon • **371.1** hast[e]ly • **371.4** blyve • **377.4** Other shyft have not wee • **378.4** saynt[e] • **381.4** I wolde vouch it safe on the • **392.1** hast[e]ly

401.4 *omit* good • **409.2** shete • **409.4** gan they mete • **412.1** Mercy then, Sayd Robin to our king *[changed by Child in addenda]* • **412.2** this *[changed by Child in addenda]* • **417.2** [wyll] come • **421.3** also i-wys • **423.1** They bente theyr bowes • **433.3** he had • **436.2** fayre • **437.3** compted• **444.4** then • **454.3** Kyrke[s]ly

Bibliography

Note: Citations in the notes are to the "short name" listed at the head of each bibliographic entry. Items are listed in the bibliography in "short name" order. A short name in ALL CAPS indicates a key source.

Barlow: Frank Barlow, *William Rufus* (one of the Yale English Monarchs series), 1983, 1990, 2000 (I use the 2000 Yale paperback edition)

Binns: Norman E. Binns, *An Introduction to Historical Bibliography,* second edition, revised, Association of Assistant Librarians, 1962

Burrow/Turville-Petre: J. A. Burrow and Thorlac Turville-Petre, *A Book of Middle English,* second edition, 1996 (I use the 1999 Blackwell edition)

CHAMBERS: E. K. Chambers, *English Literature at the Close of the Middle Ages,* Oxford, 1945, 1947

CHILD: Francis James Child, *The English and Scottish Popular Ballads,* 10 volumes. N.B. All page references to Child are to volume III of the five volume Dover edition. Includes a text of the "Gest."

CLAWSON: William Hall Clawson, *The Gest of Robin Hood*, University of Toronto Studies: Philological Series, 1909 (I use the undated Nabu Public Domain reprint, a poor-quality scan of a library copy)

DOBSON/TAYLOR: R. B Dobson and J. Taylor, *Rymes of Robyn Hood: An Introduction to the English Outlaw,* University of Pittsburg Press, 1976. Includes a text of the "Gest."

Duff-Bibliog: E(dward) Gordon Duff, *Fifteenth Century English Books: A Bibliography of Books and Documents Printed in England and of Books for the English Market Printed Abroad,* Bbliographic Society/Oxford University Press, 1907 (I use the undated Nabu scanned reprint)

Duff-Hand-List: E(dward) Gordon Duff, *Hand-Lists of English Printers 1501–1556,* Part I, Blades, East & Blades, 1895 ("Digitized by Google")

Duff-Printers: E(dward) Gordon Duff, *The Printers, Stationers, and Bookbinders of Wesminster and London from 1476 to 1535,* Cambridge University Press, 1906 ("Digitized by Google")

Gummere: Francis B. Gummere, *Old English Ballads,* Ginn & Company, 1897. Includes a text of the "Gest."

Gutch: John Mathew Gutch, editor, *A Lytell Geste of Robin Hode: With Other Ancient & Modern Ballads and Songs Relating to the Celebrated Yeoman,* volume I, Longman, Brown, Green, & Longman, 1847

Hahn: Thomas Hahn, editor, *Sir Gawain: Eleven Romances and Tales,* TEAMS (Consortium for the Teaching of the Middle Ages), Medieval Institute Publications, Western Michigan University, 1995

Hall: Louis B. Hall, *The Knightly Tales of Sir Gawain,* with introductions and translations by Hall, Nelson-Hall, 1976

Holt: J. C. Holt, *Robin Hood,* second edition, revised and enlarged, Thames & Hudson, 1989.

Isaac: Frank Isaac, *English & Scottish Printing Types 1501–35 * 1508–41,* Facsimilies and Illustrations No. II, Bibliographic Society, Oxford, 1930

Knight: Stephen Knight, editor (with a manuscript description by Hilton Kelliher), *Robin Hood: The Forresters Manuscript* (British Library Additional MS 71158), D. S. Brewer, 1998

KNIGHT/OHLGREN: Stephen Knight and Thomas Ohlgren, editors, *Robin Hood and Other Outlaw Tales,* TEAMS, Medieval Institute Publications, Western Michigan University, 2000. Portions available at http://tinyurl.com/tbdx-KnightOhlgren. Has a text of the "Gest."

LindahlEtAl: Carl Lindahl, John McNamara, John Lindow, editors, *Medieval Folklore: A Guide to Myths, Legends, Tales, Beliefs, and Customs,* Oxford, 2000, 2002

Lyon: Ann Lyon, *Constitutional History of the United Kingdom*, Cavendish Publishing, 2003

Moran: James Moran, *Wynkyn de Worde: Father of Fleet Street*, 1960, 1976; revised edition with a foreword by John Dreyfus and bibliography by Lotte Hellinga and Mary Erler published by the British Library 2003

OATES: J. C. T. Oates, "The Little Gest of Robin Hood: A Note on the Pynson and Lettersnijder Editions," *Studies in Bibliography*, Vol. 16, University of Virginia, 1963; http://tinyurl.com/tbdx-OatesGRH

Ohlgren: Thomas H. Ohlgren, editor, *Medieval Outlaws: Ten Tales in Modern English*, Sutton, 1998

OHLGREN/MATHESON: Thomas H. Ohlgren, *Robin Hood: The Early Poems, 1465–1560, Texts, Contexts, and Ideology*, with an Appendix: The Dialects and Languages of Selected Robin Hood Poems by Lister M. Matheson, University of Delaware Press, 2007

Phillips/Keatman: Graham Phillips & Martin Keatman, *Robin Hood: The Man Behind the Myth*, Michael O'Mara Books, 1995

Pollard: A. J. Pollard, *Imagining Robin Hood*, Routledge, 2004

Prestwich: Michael Prestwich, *The Three Edwards: War and State in England 1272–1377*, Weidenfeld, 1980

Steinberg/Trevitt: S. H. Steinberg, *Five Hundred Years of Printing*, 1955; revised by John Trevitt, The British Library/Oak Knoll Press, 1996

Tolkien/Gordon: J. R. R. Tolkien and E. V. Gordon, *Sir Gawain and the Green Knight*, second edition revisedby Norman Davis, Oxford, 1967

Young: Charles R. Young, *The Royal Forests of Medieval England*, University of Pennsylvania Press, 1979

Endnotes

1. Child, pp. 39-89
2. e.g. Holt, pp. 62-74
3. 1 Samuel 27:8–10
4. there are two versions of this, in 1 Samuel 24 and 26
5. Chaucer's Prioress's Tale is typical of the genre; Burrow/Turville-Petre, p. 306. For the "Gest's" Miracle, see Ohlgren/Matheson, pp. 152–153; Clawson, p. 31
6. Pollard, p. 173
7. Dobson/Taylor, p. 10
8. LindahlEtAl, p. 346
9. Dobson/Taylor, p. 33
10. Holt, p. 128
11. Holt, p. 142
12. Holt, p. 157
13. Ohlgren, p. 220
14. Ohlgren/Matheson, p. 25
15. Tolkien/Gordon, p. xxi
16. Tolkien/Gordon, p. xix; cf. Hahn, pp. 343, 348, 356 (note on line 271)
17. Hahn, p. 26
18. Prestwich3, p. 80
19. Gutch, p. 81
20. Chambers, p. 134
21. Knight/Ohlgren, p. 81
22. Holt, p. 114
23. Clawson, pp. 5-6, 128; cf. Holt, p. 192

24. Young, p. 163
25. Ohlgren, p. 217
26. Ohlgren/Matheson, p. 185
27. Burrow/Turville-Petre, p. 5
28. Dobson/Taylor, p. 6.
29. Ohlgren/Matheson, p. 210
30. Phillips/Keatman, p. 11
31. Phillips/Keatman, p. 12
32. Duff-Bibiog, p. 100
33. Oates, p. 3
34. Dobson/Taylor, p. 208
35. Gutch, p. 141
36. Oates, p. 9
37. Isaac, notes to plates 92, 93
38. Gutch, pp. 80, 142
39. Holt, p. 122
40. Isaac, introduction to Myllar and Chepman
41. Clawson, p. 2
42. Ohlgren/Matheson, p. 98
43. Binns, p. 110
44. Moran, pp. 26–38
45. Isaac, facing figure 1
46. Duff-Bibliog, pp. 127–129
47. Isaac, figure 1
48. Isaac, notes to plates 2 and 3
49. Binns, p. 109
50. Duff-Hand-List, p. 2

The Gest of Robyn Hode

51. Duff-Printers p. 131
52. Isaac, notes on Pynson
53. Oates, p. 7
54. Ohlgen/Matheson, p. 112
55. Ohlgren/Matheson, p. 117
56. Ohlgren/Matheson, pp. 117–120
57. Child, p. 40
58. Duff-Bibliog, p. 100
59. Duff-Printers, p. 23
60. Child, p. 40
61. Ohlgren/Matheson, p. 98
62. Ohlgren/Matheson, p. 126
63. Duff-Bibliog, p. 129
64. Gutch1, pp. 80, 14
65. Clawson, , p. 3; cf. Phillips/Keatman, p. 13
66. Isaac, introduction to Copland; Duff-Printers, p. 146
67. Duff-Printers, p. 7
68. Duff-Printers, p. 139
69. Ohlgren/Matheson, pp. 114-115
70. Knight, p. 7
71. Oates, pp. 5–6
72. Duff-Bibliog, p. 100
73. Isaac, preface to images 92 and 93 of the "Gest"
74. Oates, p. 4
75. Dobson/Taylor, pp. 71–72
76. Ohlgren/Matheson, p. 98
77. Isaac, notes preceding plate 13

78. Isaac, before plate 1
79. Isaac, figures 13, 14, 15, and esp. 19
80. Isaac, before plate 35
81. Isaac, before plate 45
82. Isaac, plate 47
83. Isaac, before plate 50
84. Isaac, introduction to Berthelet
85. Isaac, introduction to Byddell
86. Isaac, introduction to Herford
87. Isaac, before plate 26
88. Isaac, before plate 44
89. Isaac, before plate 36
90. Isaac, before plate 48
91. Isaac, before plate 53
92. Isaac, before plate 55
93. Isaac, introduction to Chepman and Myllar
94. Duff-Bibliog, p. ix
95. Ohlgren/Matheson, p. 101
96. Ohlgren/Matheson, p. 203
97. Ohlgren/Matheson, p. 249n.
98. Steinberg/Trevitt, p. 48
99. Binns, p. 112
100. Dobson/Taylor, p. 8
101. Oates, p. 9
102. Ohlgren/Matheson, pp. 200, 203
103. Ohlgren/Matheson, pp. 107–108
104. Ohlgren/Matheson, p. 110

105. Clawson, p. 3

106. Phillips/Keatman, p. 13

107. Ohlgren/Matheson, p. 130

108. Ohlgren/Matheson, pp. 132–133

109. Ohlgren/Matheson, p. 122

110. Child, p. 40

111. Knight/Ohlgren, p. 80

112. Ohlgren/Matheson, p. 101

113. Steinberg/Trevitt, p. 58

114. Holt, p. 69

115. Knight, p. xvii

116. Knight, pp. xxvi, 92

117. Barlow, p. 363

118. Gummere, p. 336

119. Holt, photo 15 facing p. 97; Ohlgren, p. 316 n. 9

120. Lyon, p. 166

121. Knight/Ohlgren, p. 163

CPSIA information can be obtained at www.ICGtesting.com
Printed in the USA
LVOW012330290413

331521LV00008B/216/P